Library of
Davidson College

FROM TAPE
TO PRODUCT

LIBRARY HI TECH SERIES

Number one: Automation in Libraries:
A LITA Bibliography, 1978-1982
Number two: Retrospective Conversion:
From Cards to Computer
Number three: From Tape to Product:
Some Practical Considerations on
the Use of OCLC-MARC Tapes

pierian press
1985

FROM TAPE TO PRODUCT:

Some Practical Considerations on the Use of OCLC-MARC Tapes

edited by
Barry B. Baker
University of Georgia
and
Lynne D. Lysiak
Appalachian State University

Library of Congress Catalog Card Number 85-60594
ISBN 0-87650-191-9

025.3
F931

Copyright © 1985, The Pierian Press
All Rights Reserved

86-6877

THE PIERIAN PRESS
P.O. Box 1808
Ann Arbor, MI. 48106

Contents

Introduction vii

TAPE USES AND FORMAT
    Overview of OCLC–MARC Tape Uses 1
        Richard W. Meyer
    MARC Format on Tape: A Tutorial 15
        Michele I. Dalehite

TAPE PROCESSING
    An Overview of Tape File Processing at SOLINET 39
        Richard E. James
    Processing OCLC Tapes for COM Catalog
        Production: Georgia Institute of Technology 43
        Julia Zimmerman
    Processing OCLC Tapes: Triangle Research Libraries
        Network 57
        Jeanne Sawyer

PRODUCTS: PROBLEMS AND SOLUTIONS
    COM Catalog Problems and Solutions: Georgia
        State University 65
        Christina Landram
    Implementation of a CLSI Circulation System:
        Winthrop College 71
        Laurance R. Mitlin
    OCLC and DataPhase: Public Library of Charlotte
        and Mecklenburg County 79
        Carol B. Myers
    Processing OCLC Archive Tapes for the FOCUS
        System: University of Florida 87
        Nolan F. Pope
    OCLC Tapes and the Development of a Local
        System: University of Alabama in Birmingham 99
        Jerry W. Stephens

MAINTENANCE CONSIDERATIONS
   COM Catalog Maintenance Considerations:
      Georgia State University 103
     Christina Landram
   Database Maintenance: University of Alabama
      in Birmingham 109
     Jerry W. Stephens

Selected Bibliography 113
Index 117

Introduction

Since the inception of online cataloging with OCLC in 1971, libraries have routinely been storing current cataloging information in both machine readable and manual forms. As more and more libraries progress to using their machine readable data, the possibilities, problems and solutions associated with their use are becoming evident. Consequently, librarians are becoming more aware and informed in the areas of database processing and product development using their stored data.

Machine readable data from OCLC is not just a magnetic tape mirror image of a catalog card, nor for that matter, of the OCLC screen display. All the stored transactions from cataloging do not constitute a workable database. Changes in formats, input standards and cataloging code have been made throughout the history of online cataloging. OCLC–MARC and LC–MARC do differ. Because of the visibility and current utility of the catalog card, maintenance has often been lavished upon it, while errors are allowed to languish in the machine readable file. Manual filing accommodates nuances in entries that machine filing steadfastly ignores. Local improvisation and idiosyncracies, frequently for the benefit of manual file production, and often to the detriment of the machine file, are usually poorly documented. Economics and/or ignorance often contribute to a large number of "dirty" or incomplete records in the transaction file through retrospective conversion projects.

All of the above contribute to problems in attempting to develop products from machine readable data on tape derived from OCLC cataloging, popularly termed "archive tapes." As a result, librarians are often shocked when they see the result of their cataloging procedures through the years on the machine readable records in their database.

In April, 1982 in Atlanta, Georgia, the Resources and Technical Services Section of the Southeastern Library Association presented a conference entitled, "From Tape to Product: Some Practical

Considerations," which addressed cataloging data usage. The program's audience consisted of catalogers, who store the data; administrators, who must be aware of potential uses and problems associated with the data; other library personnel involved with product development and usage; and vendor and network representatives.

The program was divided into four segments: introductory sessions addressed archive tape applications and the MARC format on tape; tape processing procedures were presented from both single and multi-institutional viewpoints; specific products were examined in light of problems and solutions encountered in development; and maintenance considerations used to keep the local database in good repair were discussed in terms of holdings, authorities and bibliographic information.

Most of the papers presented at that conference are presented herein. As with any conference proceedings, much information is regrettably lost in the form of visual presentation, such as overhead transparencies; and question-answers and discussion. We are most pleased, however, to present in one volume a comprehensive examination of product development from OCLC cataloging data.

We are especially indebted to the speakers who presented their papers and have contributed even more time to reviewing and updating them, providing information current through December, 1983. Further, thanks go to the vendors who supported the workshop with literature and representatives. Our appreciation is extended too to those members of SELA who worked to make the conference a success: Callie McGinnis of Columbus College for publicity and brochures; Joyce Cohrs of DeKalb Library System for local arrangements; and Ann Hope of the University of Georgia Libraries for registration. Last, to the staff of the Southeastern Library Network, especially Michele Dalehite, our thanks for information, support, and help with countless details in having this all come to fruition.

BBB
LDL

Overview of OCLC-MARC Tape Uses

Richard W. Meyer
Associate Director of Libraries
Clemson University

OCLC-MARC archive tapes have been used by a variety of institutions for a multitude of purposes. A brief overview of the kinds and the extent of their use is provided. From that overview, a synthesis has been attempted in order to determine the importance of the role such tapes have played in the development of library automation over the past few years. The most popular output products and some of the significant experience and problems associated with the use of OCLC tapes is covered. A suggested trend on future use for the development of databases is noted.

The intent of this paper is to provide an overview of the uses of OCLC-MARC archive tapes. A brief summary of the various ways in which these tapes have been used by libraries; of what kinds of libraries have used tapes; of the most popular output products; and of some of the problems associated with their use is given. Due to the large number of tape users and variety of uses to which they may be put, the slant is not toward a comprehensive history but to a philosophical analysis. This is appropriate because it is impossible to reduce the tremendous amount of experience which exists on archive tape use into a brief paper. It is more valuable to synthesize what is involved from a macroscopic viewpoint, and to leave the more important, specific approaches for various products to the other papers included here.

There are two papers, although published several years ago, which are pertinent in a philosophical way to what is being considered here. The first of these, written by Doralyn Hickey, was published in *LRTS* in 1967.[1] In the article titled "Bridging the gap between cataloging and information retrieval," Dr. Hickey examined the difference in roles between catalogers and information retrieval specialists.

After World War II and amidst the environment the war created for exhaustively indexed scientific information, catalogers went their unique way -- handling things with manual methods and thus providing ineffective if not worthless retrieval for scientific information. This was especially true in the case of the growing body of information published as report literature. Scientists pursued another path to create the world of documentalists or information retrieval specialists -- heavy users of automated retrieval systems.

This dichotomy continues to this day. As a result, many librarians are uneasy, if not ignorant, in the area of automation and are unable to cope with the concepts of information retrieval or machine readable records. As a solution, Dr. Hickey suggested building a temporary bridge – "the rope and vine variety" -- with several appropriate strands. Briefly, these are:

1. "a genuine interest in and enthusiasm for the future of librar--ianship, what ever direction it may take;"

2. "a program of self education" – she suggests some appropriate reading;

3. "a structured educational experience" – take a course or two as announced in *American Libraries*;

4. "the opportunity for practical work with machines and systems of information or citation retrieval."

It is this last strand in which we are currently interested. We have begun to reach the stage where the *average* librarian is getting his hands on the machine -- via OCLC, Lockheed, BRS, and so forth. And, as a result our attitudes are changing about information retrieval; about what is needed in terms of access to our collections; about machine readable records, and about what to do with these machine readable records.

The second paper was published by Herbert B. Landau in *Special Libraries* in March 1971.[2] It is titled "Can the librarian become a computer data base manager?" The answer to that question is simple. If he wants to use machine readable records, the librarian has to become a database manager. I refer you to Mr. Landau's argument and suggestions, and here only summarize what he has to say.

According to Landau, librarians' duties "involve providing assistance to users, extracting information from the database entries and providing guidance in what should be documented, in how much detail, and in what form." The first figure summa--rizes Landau's view of the job of librarian and/or database manager.

Figure 1
Landau's Database Manager Functions

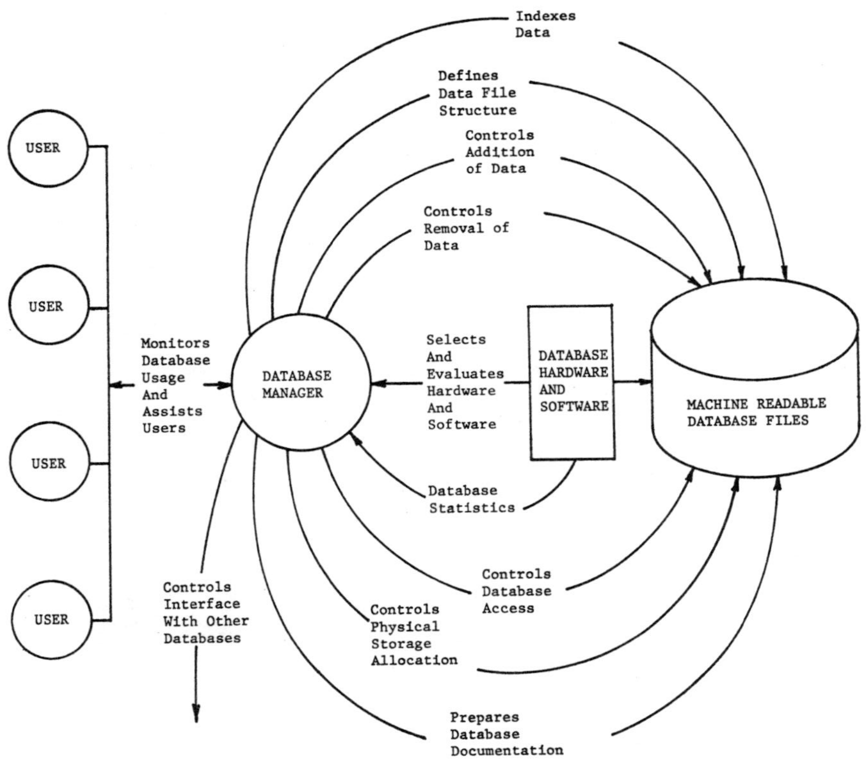

They are analogous roles.

The key in those two papers is that what is required of the librarian is that he free his thinking from the strictures of the *library* way of doing things and be adapted to the flexibility inherent in the *database managers'* way of doing things. Fortunately, the use of OCLC archive tapes provides ample opportunity for librarians to be involved in the learning experience of managing databases and in providing improved products and information services based on those databases.

Availability of OCLC Tapes

Although not widely distributed at first, archive tapes have been available to OCLC users since 1974. Originally intended as a back-up preservation method for card production, their use for other purposes has grown tremendously. The OCLC Annual Report for 1982-83 indicates that 44.3 million records were distributed on tape during that year.[3] Many of the tapes have been sent directly to user libraries, but majority currently go to the regional networks. SOLINET, for instance, has assisted in providing tape handling services and creation of various output products since 1978-79.

All of the ways in which OCLC archive tapes have been used, of course, are not described in the library literature. However, a review of the literature serves to point out many possibilities as well as evolving trends.

Archive tapes have been used experimentally in acquisitions, collection development, statistical studies, inventorying, and bibliographic projects. They have been used productively for database creation and retrospective conversion for computer output microform and printed catalogs, serials holdings lists and online circulation systems. They are also being used as an input mechanism to online catalogs.

One of the earliest experimental efforts described was reported by Glyn Evans of SUNY/OCLC in 1977.[4] Evans reported on a project based on the merging of some thirty-two thousand cataloging records from four libraries. Computer programs were used to determine whether the archive tapes could be utilized for collection development analyses. The programs successfully provided statistical analyses relevant to disciplines and overlap of holdings between one or more libraries. Comparisons of relative collection strengths among library collections were thus made available.

David Kim reported in March 1982 on an innovative approach used to develop several collection management profiles for the University of Lowell based on analysis of OCLC tapes. Efforts there involved analysis of incoming tapes to determine the subject breakdown of new acquisitions. Additional analysis determined profiles of acquisitions by type of material, contents, scholarly discipline, curriculum areas and holding library.[5]

A similar kind of effort geared to developing a technique useful for collection inventorying was reported by Barbara Pinzelik of Purdue in 1979.[6] Over many years, Purdue tried at least four different methods of inventorying to monitor book losses in the libraries. Their latest effort was based on a random sample of records extracted from three years of cumulated archive tapes. The extracted records, in the form of brief work slips, were searched against the stacks. Analysis of the search results was used successfully to pinpoint areas of the collection where significant losses were occurring. Purdue subsequently adopted this methodology for their inventory process.

In another experimental effort, a significant research study was reported by William Pringle of Carnegie Mellon, also in 1979.[7] CMU developed programs to manipulate archive tapes with the intent of building a machine readable database. One of the concerns that surfaced during this work was the effect of retaining particular MARC tags on the size of records and of the database. Their efforts resulted in a statistical analysis and algorithms which can be used to predict the effect on output products based on the choice of various options used in producing those products.

Database Creation and Maintenance

While these experiments and many others in the area of collection development and analysis have proven fruitful, the major impact of the availability of archive tapes has been in the area of database creation and maintenance. It was proposed late in 1980 by Battelle Memorial Laboratories that the tapes could be used by the bibliographic utilities to link OCLC with the RLIN, WLN and LC databases.[8]

Unfortunately, that report followed hard on the heels of a major flap over who owns the records in the utility databases.[9] OCLC requested copyright for its database and tightened restrictions on the distribution of archive records to the databases of other utilities and vendors. While that uproar has quieted somewhat, no routine transfer of tapes between networks has yet been established. The door, however, is open, and as witnessed by several RLG members who load their tapes to OCLC, there are incentives for RLIN libraries to have their records input to OCLC.

Aside from utility-to-vendor limitations, tapes are being widely used to maintain databases for individual libraries and regional networks. The output products resulting from those databases vary considerably.

Bob Holley reported on significant experience gained at Yale University by early 1979 in handling archive tapes prior to their ever having produced a product. The intent was to "create a cumulative master file in which each item cataloged is represented by only one record with correct location information and with acceptable cataloging."[10] Yale subsequently loaded this data into RLIN, and from RLIN archive tapes, produced an in-house authority index on microfiche, for about a year.[11] Yale, therefore, has developed database maintenance experience which is common to many other tape users. Some of those experiences have resulted in successful products, but perhaps more importantly many librarians are learning what database management is all about.

For instance, two projects, set up at Iowa State University to generate enhanced subject access to monographs and a reference collection, were reported by William Mischo at the ASIS meeting in 1980.[12] The title fields from archive tape records provided a string of descriptors for each title. These were manipulated utilizing computer assisted indexing techniques to generate computer output microfiche indexes. Some information on the value of title descriptors for online access to MARC records was determined by these projects.

In another case, North Carolina State University, as reported by Bill Horner in 1979, has received archive tapes since 1975. They have been merged into an offline bibliographic database.[13] From that file, they have generated reports on cataloging statistics and activity and "selected subject bibliographies using a keyphrase search of both subject and title tags." They have also created item status records for their circulation system, call number indexes to the database and error reports.

Furthermore, as part of the Triangle Universities Libraries Cooperative Committee, they have merged their database with Duke and UNC-Chapel Hill and from that file, created a master database and a COM catalog as reported by Jeanne Sawyer in 1982.[14] They have included a number of retrospective records from prior to 1975 by using the OCLC system to generate archive tape records of older holdings.

Retrospective Conversion/COM

This retrospective conversion capability of OCLC has been used well by many libraries and it is relatively common among those who create COM catalogs. INCOLSA creates a COM catalog for a number of institutions which use their processing center for small libraries.[15] AMIGOS and SOLINET have accomplished similar projects.

AMIGOS goes several steps further than most networks by providing, in addition to a COM catalog production service, other tape handling and extraction services. Their operation provides statistical analyses, serials holdings analyses, file size and average record size tallies for circulation system developments, duplicate record processing, file clean--up, and batch authority control of current files to AACR-2 form.[16] SOLINET provides very similar services and has also developed an online regional database.[17]

A number of individual libraries have also produced their own COM catalogs. The Montana State Library has been developing a system to merge OCLC archive records with WLN records to produce a union catalog for that state.[18] The New York State Library produced an elegant three volume printed catalog of state documents cataloged through OCLC by the State Library.[19]

What was probably the first use of OCLC archive tapes to produce a COM catalog was reported by John Knapp and me in 1975.[20] The experience we gathered, along with that of several others cited above, has served to isolate the procedures involved. It also has provided a mechanism for at least defining many of the problems inherent in trying to develop a database from machine readable archive tapes. Some of the other contributors to this volume will provide a thorough review of this process and the inherent snags; they will be covered only briefly here.

To produce a COM catalog, OCLC tapes require a great deal of editing, sorting and merging. *First,* OCLC tapes are coded in ASCII (American Standard Code for Information Interchange). This is fine because it is a standard. Unfortunately, IBM equipment — the most commonly used — isn't typically set up to work with ASCII code. It prefers EBCDIC (Extended Binary Coded Decimal Interchange Code). However, you can inform the computer that you are going to feed it an ASCII tape and it will know to translate this to EBCDIC before doing anything else with the data.

Unfortunately, there are a few characters used in MARC records which are defined a particular way in ASCII by OCLC but which are translated by the IBM System software into inappropriate symbols. This is because IBM used the associated decimal code to define some other character or control symbol than the one which was expected. What this means is that you have to provide a program at the front end of your catalog programs to properly interpret a few little symbols such as the end of field mark.

Second, OCLC tapes will include multiple uses of some individual OCLC records. Every time OCLC users update on a record from which they have produced or updated before, an additional copy of that record will appear on their archive tape. A program has to be able to tell which one of these copies to use. In most cases the latest use will be the one wanted, but it is possible that an earlier use is the valid record. Some allowance in procedures and programs is required to accommodate this.

Third, individual records will contain information that needs to be interpreted before it can be used. For instance, the size of books is recorded in the collation field in MARC records. OCLC card production programs match the size indicated in a record with the individual library's profile to determine if an oversize stamp is required on the catalog card. A similar accommodation is required in COM catalog production programs, otherwise users could be looking for oversize books in the wrong place.

Similarly, anything that is interpreted in card production programs also has to be interpreted in COM production. Most of these conditions can be handled by the vendor providing your catalog if you have one, however, you do have to know enough to provide him with the rules.

While these problems illustrate some of the difficulties associated with the development of products generated from OCLC tapes, there are certainly benefits. The use of an experienced vendor with flexible software capable of generating catalogs in a number of varieties and formats presents great potential for improving services to users.

Advantages of COM

Many libraries will desire a more or less traditional catalog. This could be a divided author, title, subject catalog which looks essentially just like a card catalog. Even so, because of the automation involved, a COM catalog can be generated with less hassle and expense than a card catalog and be worthwhile on that basis. However, it is possible, indeed desirable, to take advantage of our technology to produce some variations. For example, it is possible to create a name catalog, or a publishers catalog, or a key-word catalog, or a chronological catalog, or a form of media catalog. These can all be accomplished and some have been demonstrated.

For instance, Blackwell/North America created for one Texas library a subject catalog which was subfiled, not by author, but by reverse chronological sequence instead. What's more, if any particular sequence is determined to be unacceptable, it's possible to change the output product very readily.

Returning to the author sequence from chronological sequence requires only a minor program change. Numberless hours of effort would be required for a similar change in a card catalog. What I've just mentioned represents one of the advantages of the COM catalog over the card catalog. There are other advantages which I have elaborated on elsewhere.[21] There are also some disadvantages of COM, but the technology offers us the opportunity to gain database experience relevant to the development of more advanced systems.

Many libraries have in recent years found the archive tapes a convenient means to add records to files which support online circulation systems and online catalogs. Barbara Case and others have reported on the use of archive tapes in the California State Universities and Colleges' CLSI circulation system.[22] Ohio State University, Virginia Polytechnic Institute, Oral Roberts University, University of Nebraska--Lincoln, University of Alabama--Birmingham and many others regularly have used or use archive tapes to update the files of their online circulation systems.[23]

Some of those systems provide not only for circulation, but they are evolving into online catalogs and integrated bibliographic support systems. UCLA and the University of California System have demonstrated prototype, online catalogs, as has Dartmouth College.[24] The library at the University of Georgia has operated an online technical services support system for several years into which they input archive tapes.[25] Pennsylvania State University operates similarly.[26]

However, as these systems continue to evolve, their managers have found it convenient to improve the data transmission link. They are replacing the use of archive tapes as a data transmission technique with direct links between OCLC terminals and other hardware.

Oral Roberts University has installed hardware which interfaces the OCLC terminal print--port to their turnkey circulation system. Records are searched on the OCLC system and when matched against the book in hand, the cataloging record is produced. It is then reformatted, edited with local holdings information, and transmitted to the circulation hardware. Tarrant County Junior College near Fort Worth does the same thing, but into their own IBM system.

Several turnkey vendors have been marketing hardware supported interfaces for linkage of the OCLC terminal to their systems since 1979.[27] This approach currently is used by many turnkey customers. Central State in Oklahoma and Clemson University have linked their OCLC terminals to their main campus computers through in--house terminals, to allow updating of their databases running under NOTIS. Additional linkages between various systems are being announced frequently.[28]

The fact that these linkages are beginning to appear is because of an evolving technology which is made possible, in part at least, by the cumulative database maintenance experience afforded by utilization of OCLC--MARC archive tapes. What this means is not thoroughly clear, but there certainly seem to be some historical implications.

Books, Cards, Computer

During the two decades immediately preceding the turn of the century, a significant transition took place in the way libraries recorded their holdings. For a few thousand years libraries had commonly provided access to their collections by simply making a list of their holdings. There were refinements of that technique, but it wasn't until the industrial revolution and coinciding events, such as an explosion of literature, that a new system was required to help users locate the material they needed. A brilliant innovation resulted.

The work of Cutter, Panizzi, Jewett and others culminated in a standardized way of organizing collections which utilized 3 x 5 cards and a set of logical principles for organizing materials. A marvelous tool called the card catalog resulted because of the power of dictionary filing and LC's printed card service. It was flexible, rigorous, timely and effective. You could make additions and changes on a daily basis which provided an instantaneous update on the condition of the collection. It was consistent because logical rules made it so. It was effective because it did the job.

Today, however, we are in the midst of another revolution. We have a new explosion of literature. We have a rapidly changing technology. We have a change from the industrial society to what some have called the communications age. With what we will eventually level off, is as yet unclear.

Future shock and changing social values have had victimizing effects in every area. The card catalog is also a victim. It is no longer the most effective tool. In response to the diminishing effectiveness of the card catalog, librarians have turned to technology. With the computer, the ease and flexibility of providing access to material is greatly enhanced. It is possible to provide very handy, reproducible printed lists and indexes, but these are slow and expensive.

The use of the computer and OCLC archive tapes to produce COM catalogs and similar products represents a convenient choice of alternatives during a period of technological change. This period of change is providing us with both a learning experience and the potential for tremendous bibliographic innovation. As librarians learn to become database managers, that potential will be realized. The result will be a solid bridge into the best possible new world of libraries for library users.

REFERENCES

1. Hickey, Doralyn J. "Bridging the gap between cataloging and information retrieval" *LRTS* 11:173–183 (Spring 1967).

2. Landau, Herbert B. "Can the librarian become a computer data base manager?" *Special Libs* 62/8:117–124 (March 1971).

3. OCLC. *1982–83 Annual Report* (Columbus: 1983).

4. Evans, Glyn T., Roger Gifford, and Donald R. Franz. *Collection development analysis using OCLC archival tapes* (Albany: State University of New York. University Libraries, 1977) ED 152299. See also: Moore, Barbara, Tamara J. Miller and Donald L. Tolliver. "Title overlap: a study of duplication in the University of Wisconsin System Libraries" *College and Research Libraries* 1/1:14–21 (January 1982).

5. Kim, David. "OCLC–MARC tapes and collection management" *ITAL* 1/1:22–27 (March 1982).

6. Pinzelik, Barbara. *Monitoring book losses in a large academic library: four methods* (West Lafayette, Ind: Purdue University Libraries, 1979) ED 203852.

7. Pringle, William R. "Computing the effective length of a MARC tag" *JOLA* 12/4:387–390 (December 1979).

8. Smalley, Donald A., et al. *Linking the bibliographic utilities: benefits and costs* (Columbus: Battelle Memorial Laboratories, November 1980) ED 195276.

9. "OCLC tape users demand rights" *Amer Libs* 11/3:140, 142 (March 1980).

10. Holley, Robert P. and Dale Flecker. "Processing OCLC MARC subscription tapes at Yale University" *JOLA* 12/1:88–91 (March 1979).

11. Weisbrod, David [Telephone conversation, November 1983].

12. Mischo, William H. "Expanded access to library collections using computer assisted indexing techniques" In: American Society for Information Science, *Communicating information: proceedings of the 43rd ASIS annual meeting, 1980, v. 17, Anaheim, California, October 5–8, 1980* (NY: Knowledge Industry Publications, 1980) p 155–157.

13. Horner, William C. "Processing OCLC MARC subscription tapes at North Carolina State University" *JOLA* 12/1:91–94 (March 1979).

14. Sawyer, Jeanne. "An archive tape processing system for the Triangle Research Libraries Network" *LRTS* 26/4:362–369 (October/December, 1982).

15. Stockey, Edward A. *Retrospective conversion and index to holdings project: final report* (Indianapolis: INCOLSA, 1979).

16. Amigos Bibliographic Council, Inc. *Que Pasa?* 3/4:1 (December 1981) and 4/1:3 (September 1982).

17. Southeastern Library Network, Inc. *SOLINEWS* 9/4:6 (June 1981) and 11/2:6–7 (September 1983).

18. Matthews, Joseph R. *Resources sharing in Montana: a study of interlibrary loan and alternatives for a Montana union catalog* (Helena: Montana State Library, 1980) ED 198821.

19. New York State Library. *Dictionary catalog of official publications of the State of New York* (Albany: 1978) ED 197760.

20. Meyer, Richard W. and John F. Knapp. "COM catalog based on OCLC records" *JOLA* 8/4:312–321 (December 1975).

21. Meyer, Richard W. *Computer output microfilm and library catalogs* (Terre Haute: Indiana State University. Library, 1978) ED 156143.

22. Case, Barbara, et al. *CSUC Standard for the CLSI expanded title record* (Los Angeles: California State Universities and Colleges, Library Systems Project, 1981) ED 200248.

23. Bausser, Jaye. "Online catalogs" *RTSD Newsletter* 6/4:43

(July/August 1981) 6/5:55 (September/October 1981) and 7/1:7 (January/February 1982).

24. Fayen, Emily Gallup. *Experimental online catalog for the Dartmouth College Libraries* (Hanover, NH: Dartmouth College Libraries, 1980) ED 190145.

25. Christoffersson, John G. "Automation at the University of Georgia Libraries" *JOLA* 12/1:22–38 (March 1979).

26. Bausser, Jaye. "Online catalogs" *RTSD Newsletter* 6/6:65 (November/December 1981).

27. CL Systems, Inc. *CLSI Newsletter* No. 12:12 (Fall–Winter 1979).

28. "Interface units unveiled for libraries" *Advanced Technology/Libraries* 10/8:8–9 (August 1981).

MARC Format on Tape: A Tutorial

Michele I. Dalehite
Project Analyst
SOLINET

An introduction to the concept of the MARC communications format is presented. The following topics are addressed: data element units; data characters; fixed and variable length fields and records; the MARC record structure and its components; limitations and capabilities of the data found on OCLC-MARC tapes; and general guidelines for entering into a project requiring OCLC-MARC tape processing.

Introduction

The following information was presented in tutorial fashion at the SELA sponsored workshop "From Tape to Product: Some Practical Considerations." This tutorial was intended to make the participants aware of the MARC Communications Format and the medium in which it is used, as well as informing the participants of the differences between it and the format more familiar to them, the OCLC screen display. Since many of the participants were not familiar with basic data processing concepts and terminology, the session began with an introduction to both.

Every user of OCLC's Cataloging Subsystem has been creating tape versions of the records they use in the OCLC database. Every PRODUCE, UPDATE, ALL PRODUCE, CANCEL, and REPLACE transaction under both cataloging and retrospective conversion authorization numbers causes a record to be put on the OCLC daily archival file. It is from this archival file that OCLC generates the offline products: cards, accession lists, and subscription tapes. Many users have been receiving subscription tapes or have had them acquired by their state agencies or regional networks for union file purposes. It is these tapes that we want to discuss.

Before getting into a technical discussion of OCLC-MARC tapes, it is recommended that all prospective users of this tape data acquire the document *OCLC-MARC Subscription Service Documentation,* 4th edition, 1981, which is available from OCLC. One copy is provided with each subscription to the tape service. Additional copies can be purchased from OCLC. This document describes the physical tape product and identifies all of the data elements now found in OCLC/MARC records.

A second document, *MARC Formats for Bibliographic Data,* 1980, can be acquired from the Library of Congress. This manual describes the data elements that are currently standard. There is also a section which describes past practices and obsolete usage. LC has a subscription update service that provides replacement pages for corrections, changes, and additions to the MARC format which can keep you abreast of changes OCLC will be making. This can be critical when you have programs that may be affected by new data elements.

The Data Elements

Machine readable data are composed of collections or groupings of data elements which form logical units. The smallest unit is the BIT which is an electrical impulse registering an on/off, yes/no condition. At the other end of the spectrum is the DATABASE, a unit which may be the ultimate goal of most users of OCLC-MARC data. Between these two extremes are subunits known as *Bytes* (i.e., *Characters*), *Fields, Records,* and *Files.* As multiple elements are combined they formulate the next larger unit in the hierarchy.

The bit by itself can convey only limited information since it can register only two values: on/yes or off/no. By grouping bits together we can expand the amount of information that can be communicated. The units created by grouping bits together are called bytes. A byte can be equivalent to a character.

Through the years different standards have been used to regulate the number of bits needed to make a byte. One standard used for OCLC-MARC data is eight bits per byte. The 8-bit byte is referred to as a binary character. With 8 bits there can be 256 characters starting with 0000 0000 as the lowest and extending to 1111 1111 as the highest. In between is every possible permutation of 0's and 1's.

After grouping bits together to make bytes (i.e., characters), bytes can be grouped to make fields. Fields are predefined to have specific meaning by the programs that use the data. They can describe such things as an author's name, a subject heading, or a call number. They can be either fixed or variable fields.

Fixed fields retain a constant size usually with rigidly prescribed data content whereas variable fields have no prescribed length or content. For this reason, variable fields offer the greater

Figure 1
Data Elements

BIT	SMALLEST UNIT OF INFORMATION

It has two states: 0 or 1 (yes or no)

CHARACTER (BYTE)	GROUP OF BITS WHICH ARE TREATED AS A UNIT

OCLC--MARC data uses 8 bits per character. A-Z; 0-9; punctuation, special characters; diacritics; control characters (e.g., delimiters)

FIELD	GROUP OF CHARACTERS THAT CONSTITUTE A LOGICAL UNIT

Two types: fixed and variable
    Fixed: 001, 007, 008
    Variable: 245, 300, 590

RECORD	GROUP OF FIELDS THAT CONSTITUTE A LOGICAL UNIT

The description of one bibliographic item.

FILE	GROUP OF RECORDS THAT CONSTITUTE A LOGICAL UNIT

An institution's OCLC–MARC transaction records.

DATABASE	GROUP OF FILES THAT CONSTITUTE A LOGICAL UNIT

e.g., Bibliographic File
    Authority File
    Patron Name File
    Serials Control File
    Indices to all Files

challenge in data manipulation. It is also the reason why quality control during data entry is so critical to the integrity of this data.

The next unit in the hierarchy is the record; fields grouped together to create a logical unit. A record could describe employee personnel information, a banking transaction, or a bibliographic item. The record is the unit with which we are most concerned in OCLC–MARC tape processing.

A file is a group of records which have a common purpose. All of an institution's OCLC–MARC transactions comprise a file that represents its OCLC cataloging activities, but the file is not necessarily a representation of its catalog. Only by processing and refining that file can it represent a catalog. Such a file is also a simple form of a database, but it has limited access. Usually sorted by OCLC number, records can be retrieved only by starting at the beginning of the file and reading each record until reaching the record desired.

When files of records are stored in an online mode with separate index files and related files composed of authority, acquisition, holdings and circulation records, then we can say we have a useful database. This form of a database is a goal toward which the creation and maintenance of OCLC–MARC records is usually a critical step.

The Data Characters

If data begins with the bit, how do we form letters, numbers, punctuation marks, and diacritics from them? Remember that in an 8–bit system we get 256 unique combinations. At one time in the development of data processing each computer manufacturer assigned its own values to each binary combination. There was usually some similarity between them for the common characters such as uppercase letters, numbers and common punctuation marks. For the less common characters, however, there was enough disparity to cause considerable difficulty in communicating data between computer users. This situation led to the development of standards that would insure that the binary combinations would have the same meaning. Picture the difficulty in trying to say "hello" if computers saw the following binary displays differently:

Byte	Computer A	Computer B
0110 1000	h	ae combined
0110 0101	e	Turkish i lowercase
0110 1100	l	%
0110 1100	l	%
0110 1111	o	?

This would be the result if you confused the two primary standards: ASCII and EBCDIC. ASCII is short for American Standard Code for Information Interchange. EBCDIC is the acronym for Extended Binary Coded Decimal Interchange Code.

The OCLC–MARC tapes you receive are in an extended form of ASCII which makes provision for the special characters and diacritics used in cataloging. Many computers do not process data in ASCII but rather use EBCDIC. For these computers, the data received from OCLC must be passed through a conversion program which will convert the binary characters from ASCII to an extended form of EBCDIC.

Since the character requirements for cataloging data are greater than for most other computer applications, some computer systems do not have the ability to handle the extended forms of either ASCII or EBCDIC. In this case many of the special characters and diacritics may be lost in the conversion. Once they are lost (i.e., purged) from the records, they can never be recovered without going back to the original OCLC–MARC tapes. You should determine whether your vendor or campus computer facility can handle the additional characters.

Not all binary characters have a display character and not all line–printers can print the entire character set. For most people, reading binary characters can be tedious if not impossible. To make it easier, each binary character has been assigned a HEX value. This hex value is constant regardless of the character set used (i.e., ASCII or EBCDIC).

The binary value is split into two groups of four digits with each group given a character representation based on the binary value of that group. For example, the binary 0000 0000 is given a hex of 00 since each group of four is worth zero. 0000 0001 equals 01; 0000 0010 equals 02; and so forth. Figure 2 illustrates the pattern of hex value assignments. Figure 3 compares ASCII and EBCDIC character representation.

Even with 256 characters to work with, there are not enough to handle all of those used by OCLC. The extra characters are grouped into three extended character sets: greek letters, superscripts, and subscripts. It requires at least five physical characters to encode one extended character on tape. The first character (HEX 1B) identifies that the data is going into an extended character set. The second letter identifies which character set is being used. HEX 67 (letter g in ASCII) identifies that a greek letter will follow. HEX 62 (letter b) and HEX 70 (letter p) identify subscript and superscript respectively. The hex values following the second one are for the actual characters that are keyed into the terminal;

Figure 2
Binary-Hex Representation

DECIMAL	BINARY	HEX	DECIMAL	BINARY	HEX
0	0000 0000	00	16	0001 0000	10
1	0000 0001	01	17	0001 0001	11
2	0000 0010	02	18	0001 0010	12
3	0000 0011	03	19	0001 0011	13
4	0000 0100	04	.	.	.
5	0000 0101	05	31	0001 1111	1F
6	0000 0110	06	.	.	.
7	0000 0111	07	45	0010 1101	2D
8	0000 1000	08	.	.	.
9	0000 1001	09	70	0100 0110	46
10	0000 1010	0A	.	.	.
11	0000 1011	0B	122	0111 1010	7A
12	0000 1100	0C	.	.	.
13	0000 1101	0D	185	1011 1000	B8
14	0000 1110	0E	.	.	.
15	0000 1111	0F	256	1111 1111	FF

Figure 3
ASCII/EBCDIC Comparison

CHARACTER	ASCII		EBCDIC	
	HEX	BINARY	HEX	BINARY
A	41	0100 0001	C1	1100 0001
B	42	0100 0010	C2	1100 0010
C	43	0100 0011	C3	1100 0011
.	.	.	.	.
.	.	.	.	.
.	.	.	.	.
Z	5A	0101 1010	E9	1110 1001
.	.	.	.	.
a	61	0110 0001	81	1000 0001
b	62	0110 0010	82	1000 0010
c	63	0110 0011	83	1000 0011
.	.	.	.	.
.	.	.	.	.
.	.	.	.	.
z	7A	0111 1010	A9	1010 1001
.	.	.	.	.
0	30	0011 0000	F0	1111 0000
1	31	0011 0001	F1	1111 0001
2	32	0011 0010	F2	1111 0011
.	.	.	.	.
.	.	.	.	.
9	39	0011 1001	F2	1111 1001
.	.	.	.	.
space	20	0010 0000	40	0100 0000
delimeter	1F	0001 1111	1F	0001 1111
#	23	0010 0011	7B	0111 1011
$	24	0010 0100	5B	0101 1011
&	26	0010 0110	50	0101 0000

"a" for alpha, "b" for beta, "c" for gamma, "0–9", "+", and "–". Once the extended characters are finished, then HEX 1B is repeated followed by HEX 73 (letter s) for the return to the standard character set. Therefore, to record the Greek character "alpha" on tape, we need the following five hex values: 1B 67 61 1B 73. This characteristic of OCLC–MARC data is one for which programmers must make allowances, otherwise the hex values would be treated literally.

The Tape Medium

Before we get into the actual data itself, let us briefly review the medium on which this data is stored. Typically it is on one or more reels of magnetic tape. The tape is one--half inch wide and it has nine tracks. Eight tracks contain the eight bits of a byte with the ninth being a parity bit which is used to test the accuracy of the first eight bits. The parity bit can be compared to a check digit in an ISBN. The number of rows of bits in one inch determines your BPI (i.e., 800 or 1600 bits per inch). CPI (characters per inch) is another way of referring to this characteristic. A record on an OCLC–MARC tape is simply a collection of rows of these on/off bits, each row comprising a character. See Figure 4 for an illustration of a character on tape.

As was mentioned earlier, fields can be either fixed or variable length. OCLC–MARC records use both types. Variable length fields can vary in size, but must be at least six characters long: two indicators, a two character subfield code, at least one character in the field, and the end--of--field mark. The upper limit is usually determined by the limitations of the system on which the records are created. Fixed length fields have a pre--defined size. The advantage in programming for fixed length fields is that you always know where the data resides. In other words, position 12 of the field always retains the same function regardless of the value placed in it.

The programming differences for fixed and variable fields can be likened to tallying questionnaires in which answers are always in the same place on every page versus ones in which answers may be in different places on the page or even on different pages. Your ability to see the data quickly is reduced and in fact your ability to recognize the data when you see it may be impaired.

For computer data, this requires searching through records looking for data that is not always in the same place and recogniz-- ing that the data is applicable once it is retrieved. It is for this reason that accuracy in tags, indicators, and subfields is so critical. What the human eye can recognize at a glance, the computer must

Figure 4
Tape Representation

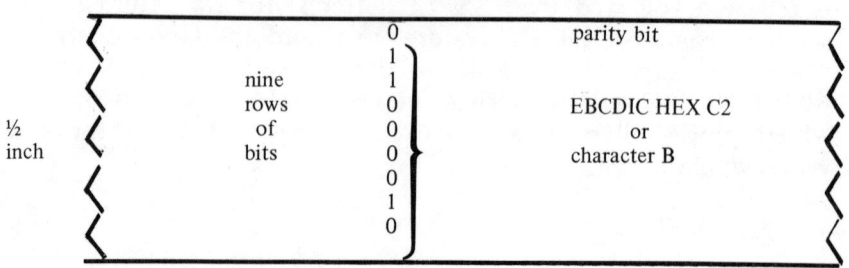

one byte or character
8 bits plus 1 parity bit

Figure 5
Variable vs. Fixed Length Records

VARIABLE

6 OCLC records:	1	1032 bytes
	2	936 bytes
	3	526 bytes
	4	2693 bytes
	5	836 bytes
	6	724 bytes
6 IRG's @ 960		5760 bytes
TOTAL		12507 bytes

L1	IRG	L2	IRG	L3	IRG	L4	IRG	L4	IRG	L5	IRG	L6
1032	960	936	960	526	960	2048	960	645	960	836	960	724

FIXED

6 OCLC records converted to 10 fixed length records	9000 bytes
1 IRG @ 960	960 bytes
TOTAL	9960 bytes

L1 p1	L1 p2	L2 p1	L2 p2	L3	L4 p1	IRG	L4 p2	L4 p3	L5	L6
900	900	900	900	900	900	960	900	900	900	900

recognize through a laborious process of condition testing. Is this the 100 tag? Is this a subfield delimiter? If so, is this the subfield a?

In addition to (or rather because of) fields being variable in length, OCLC–MARC records can vary in length: from 12 to 4096 characters. Between each record on a tape is an interrecord gap (IRG) that allows the computer to pause while it is processing the previous record. An IRG is about 5/8 inch long or the equiva-- lent of 960 characters. This requirement can consume valuable space on a magnetic tape.

Most computer systems cannot handle variable length physical records. For this reason they have to be converted to fixed length physical records. The actual length of the data describing the bibliographic item remains the same. This is called the logical record. However, the logical record is stored in physical records of consistent length with short records padded with blanks to make them long enough. By judicious choice of an optimum record size and by grouping multiple fixed length records into a block of records thereby reducing the number of IRG's needed, a significant savings in storage requirements can be realized.

An an example, the average length of OCLC–MARC records is approximately 900 characters. By changing the physical record size to 900 characters, most logical records could fit in one physical record. Those that did not might require two or more physical records. If the logical records were less than 900 characters long, they were filled with blanks to pad them out.

The savings on tape space was achieved by grouping six physical records together into a group known as a block with no IRG's between the six physical records. This reduced the number of IRG's needed. Standard 1600 bpi tapes received from OCLC contain approximately 20,000 logical records, but approximately 34,000 logical records can be stored using a 900 character, block 6 configuration. Figure 5 illustrates this savings.

One final characteristic of the records on the OCLC–MARC tapes is that the records are ordered chronologically based on the date and time they were generated through the produce or update keys. In most applications, the records must be re–sorted by OCLC number first, then in some sequential order within OCLC number to facilitate new records being merged with or compared against existing files.

The MARC Structure

The OCLC–MARC record is composed of four basic compo–

nents: the leader, the directory, the control fields, and the variable fields.

The Leader

The LEADER is the first component encountered in the record. It also contains the data that informs the programs about what kind of record is being processed. It categorizes and defines the record. The leader is 24 characters long beginning with position 0 and ending with position 23. The first five characters of the leader give the length of the logical record which is the key to reading any variable length record since it tells the program how many of the characters (i.e., bytes) that follow belong to this record. This data element does not appear in the OCLC screen display of the record.

The next three elements do display, but as part of the Fixed Field display. Position 5 is the record status code. It identifies whether the record is new, revised, or deleted. Position 6 (record type) categorizes the item as being printed language, music, film, map, or manuscript, while position 7 (bibliographic level) identifies it as being a monograph, serial, analytic, or collection. Positions 6 and 7 are used together to identify the type of material being described by the record.

Positions 8 and 9 are blank because they are not yet defined. Since this is a fixed length field, these positions are always present even though they serve no function. In a variable length field there would not be any predefined positions which would be present regardless of the individual requirements of the record.

Position 10 is an indicator count. This does not give the number of indicators in the record, but the number in each field. It is always set to 2, but the existence of this data element means that the option has been left open for increasing the number of indicators used in a record or in the MARC format. This is something programmers and developers of systems using MARC data must bear in mind; the format was designed to be flexible and it could change.

Position 11 is a subfield count. Like the indicator count it does not identify the number of subfields in the record, but rather the number of characters necessary to encode a subfield. The value is always 2, one for the delimiter mark and one for the letter or number following. Also, like the indicator count, it could be increased.

Positions 12 through 16 give the base address of data. This value is the combined length of the leader and the directory and identifies the position of the beginning of the first field in the record. This element tells the program where to start looking for actual bibliographic data.

The next two positions appear in the screen display as part of the Fixed Field. Position 17 (encoding level) identifies the level of quality of the cataloging data. Position 18 (descriptive level) records the cataloging rules used for the descriptive portion of the data: i.e., ISBD, non–ISBD, AACR2, etc.

Position 19 is blank because it is not yet defined. Position 20 gives the length of the length of the field. This value is set at 4 which means that fields cannot exceed 9999 characters because you cannot have a length that exceeds four digits. If the value were to be changed to 5, the length would then increase to 99999. However most systems have internal limits on field sizes which require them to be considerably smaller than 9999 characters.

Position 21 is the length of starting character position. Set to 5, this element identifies the number of characters that are needed to represent the starting position of a field. With a length of 5, it cannot exceed 99999. In other words, the starting character of a field in a record cannot be position 100000.

Position 22 is an undefined position in the LC–MARC format, but OCLC has defined this position to be the transaction type code. This code identifies whether the record was created from a PRODUCE, ALL PRODUCE, UPDATE, CANCEL, or REPLACE transaction. There is no character representation for this position; it is a hex value which means that in order to determine the transaction type you must have a printout of the record that shows the hex values. The hex values are:

Produce	01	Replace	11
Update	02	All produce	50
Cancel	03		

Transaction codes are discussed in more detail below. Position 23 is undefined, but the value is always set to zero rather than blank, meaning that the last character of the leader is always a zero.

The Directory

The second basic component of a MARC record is the roadmap to the record since it identifies all of the fields that record contains. This component is the DIRECTORY. Its contents consist solely of three elements: tags, lengths of fields, and starting character positions of fields. These three elements are repeated for each fixed and variable field. The first element (position 0-2) is the tag number; the next (position 3-6) is the number of characters in the field; the last (position 7-11) identifies where the first character of the field is located in the record. The starting position is also known as the "relative position" since it is accurate only in relation to the base address found in the leader.

A program that manipulates MARC records scans the directory until it finds the desired tag. It now knows the starting character position and how long the field is so it can find where the field ends. A program can determine how many fields are in a record, what the average length of the fields are, and the presence or absence of fields by reading the directory and processing the data found in it.

In OCLC-MARC tapes, the tags in the directory are listed in the same order that the fields appear in the record. Some other suppliers of MARC data re--arrange the tags to be in strict numerical order. The fields, however, remain in the order of input. This difference can be critical if your program assumes that the directory will always be ordered one way or the other.

The Control Fields

The third component of MARC records is a set of fields called CONTROL FIELDS. Control fields are basically fixed fields which means that they maintain a constant length with each character having a constant function. However, changes in length and function have occurred in recent years which make older and newer records different. These differences either have to be allowed for or older records have to be programmatically changed to conform to current requirements. The MARC format defines nine control fields between tags 001 and 009, but only five are used at this time: 001, 005, 007, 008, and 009.

The 001 or Record Control Number field contains the OCLC control number in OCLC-MARC records and the LC card number in LC-MARC records. The format of the 001 OCLC-MARC field is:

Position 0-2   Prefix: ocm; ocl (pre 80/07/01)
Position 3-10   Control number; right justified, zero filled
Position 11   Blank
Position 12   End of field mark (HEX 1E in ASCII and EBCDIC)

The OCLC prefix has been changed. Originally it was "ocl" with an 8-digit number that began with the digit 7. In anticipation of record 10,000,000 the prefix was changed to "ocm" with the

Figure 6
Leader

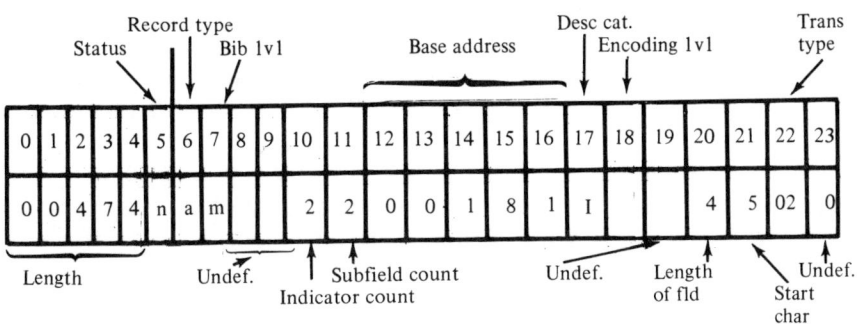

Figure 7
Directory

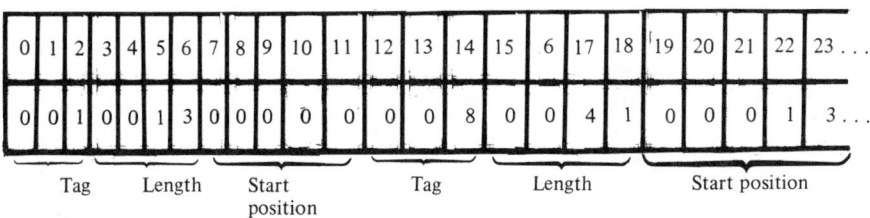

8-digit number beginning with zero. This change is critical if you are processing old and new records together. The full 8 digits of the numbers will not be compatible. To be safe, old records should be converted to change the prefix "oc17" to "ocm0."

Another change in the 001 field occurred between June 30, 1980 and June 26, 1983. During this period, the transaction date was recorded in positions 12-17 in the YYMMDD format. Position 18 then became the end--of--field mark.

OCLC began using the 005 field on June 26, 1983 for the transaction date and time. The data is recorded as YYMMDDhhmmss.0 in positions 0-13 of the field. Position 14 is the end--of--field mark. This data is supplied by the OCLC system at the time the produce or update key is used.

The 007 or Physical Description Fixed Field was originally defined for AV and Sound Recordings. It now can be used for all formats. The number of positions used varies in each format, but the length remains constant. OCLC screen displays place each position in a separate subfield, but the data is actually stored on tape as one continuous field with no indicators, subfields, or spaces between the elements. It is by the position of the characters that their function is determined. The length of the field, the function of the positions, and the acceptable values of several of the positions were changed in 1981. This means that older and newer records are not compatible.

The 008 or Fixed Field is used in all formats. It appears in the OCLC screen record as a series of data element names and associated values. The names and number of elements varies with each format. However, in the tape record the field is one continuous field of 40 characters plus an end of field character. Not all positions are defined for each format. Those that aren't contain blanks. It's only by the position of the characters that the function is known. For example, positions 0-5 record the date the record was first put into machine--readable format and positions 15-17 contain the country of publication code. In January 1981, the acceptable values for many of the fixed fields elements were changed to make usage consistent from element to element and among formats. This change makes 008 fields for pre-- and post--January 1981 records different. Usage of one of the two documents referenced in the introduction is mandatory in manipulating the 008 field.

The 009 Archival Physical Description Fixed Field is similar to the 007 field in function and format. It is only used for bibliographic items that are archival in nature.

The Variable Fields

Figure 8
Control Field

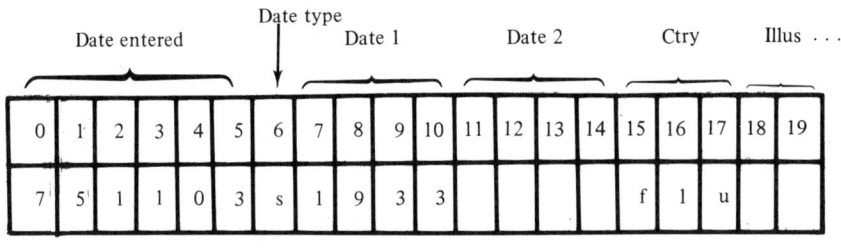

Figure 9
OCLC-MARC Screen Display Record

```
OCLC: 1801174      Rec stat: n  Entrd: 751103
Type: a   Bib  lvl: m    Govt pub:       Lang: eng   Source:        Illus:
Repr:     Enc  lvl: I    Conf pub: 0     Ctry: flu   Dat tp: s      M/F/B: 10
Indx: 0   Mod rec:       Festschr: 0     Cont:
Desc:     Int  lvl:      Dates: 1933,
010       33-0307 ?
040       dlc ‡c FUG
035       c
050   _   JS1101.M5 ‡b A4 1929
099       F.2 ‡a M61 ‡a C ‡a 1933
049   00  FUGF
110   10  Miami, Fla. ‡b Charters.
245   1_  [Charter of] the city of Miami, Florida.
260   0   [Miami?] ‡c 1933.
300       1 p. ?., v-xix, 6 1 p. ‡c 23 cm.
651   0   Charters ‡x Florida
```

Figure 10   OCLC–MARC Tape Format Record

```
        000102030405  060708091011  121314151617  181920212223  242526272829
000     30303437346E  616D20203232  303031363949  202034350230  303031303031
         0 0 4 7 4 n   a m     2 2   0 0 1 8 1 I         4 5 ? 0   0 0 1 0 0 1
030     333030303030  303038303034  313030303133  303130303031  383030303534
         3 0 0 0 0 0   0 0 8 0 0 4   1 0 0 0 1 3   0 1 0 0 0 1   8 0 0 0 5 4
060     303430303031  333030303732  303335303030  363030303835  303530303032
         0 4 0 0 0 1   3 0 0 0 7 2   0 3 5 0 0 0   6 0 0 0 8 5   0 5 0 0 0 2
090     333030303931  303939303032  323030313134  303439303030  393030313336
         3 0 0 0 9 1   0 9 9 0 0 2   2 0 0 1 1 4   0 4 9 0 0 0   9 0 0 1 3 6
120     313130303032  373030313435  323435303034  353030313732  323630303032
         1 1 0 0 0 2   7 0 0 1 4 5   2 4 5 0 0 4   5 0 0 1 7 2   2 6 0 0 0 2
150     303030323137  333030303033  343030323337  363530303032  313030323631
         0 0 0 2 1 7   3 0 0 0 0 3   4 0 0 2 3 7   6 5 1 0 0 2   1 0 0 2 7 1
180     1E6F636C3731  383031313734  201E37353131  303373313933  332020202066
           o c l 7 1   8 0 1 1 7 4          7 5 1 1   0 3 s 1 9 3   3             f
210     6C7520202020  202020202020  203030303130  20656E672020  1E20201F6120
         l u                                0 0 0 1 0     e n g         a
240     202033333030  393330372000  1E20201F6164  6C631F634655  471E20201F61
                3 3 0 0   9 3 0 7 ?           a d   l c   c F U   G             a
270     631E7C201F61  4A5331313031  2E4D351F6241  342031393239  1E20201F6146
         c _         a   J S 1 1 0 1   . M 5   b A   4     1 9 2 9               a F
300     2E321F614D36  311F61431F61  313933331E30  301F61465547  461E31301F61
         . 2     a M 6   1     a C     a   1 9 3 3   0 0     a F U G   F   1 0     a
330     4D69616D692C  20466C612E1F  624368617274  6572732E1E30  7C1F615B4368
         M i a m i ,       F l a .   b C h a r t   e r s .   0   _   a   C h
360     617275657220  6F665D207468  652063697479  206F66204D69  616D692C2046
         a r t e r       o f         t h e     c i t y       o f     M i   a m i ,     F
390     6C6F72696461  2E1E30201F61  5B4D69616D69  3F5D1F633139  33332E1E2020
         l o r i d a   .     0     a   [ M i a m i   ? ]   c 1 9   3 3 .
420     1F613120702E  20BE2E2C2076  2D7869782C20  36203120702E  1F633233636D
         a 1     p .       ¾ . ,   v   - x i x ,     6     1   p .       c 2 3 c m
450     2E1E20301F61  436861727465  72731F78466C  6F726964611D
         .     0     a   C h a r t e   r s   x F l   o r i d a
```

The last component of a MARC record is the VARIABLE FIELD GROUP. The number and type of variable fields found in bibliographic records varies from format to format. The only constant is that every record must have a title (i.e., 245) field. No other field is constant in all records because of either inapplicability to all formats or differences in standards at the time the record was created.

Figure 9 illustrates an OCLC–MARC record in the OCLC screen display. Figure 10 illustrates the same record in the OCLC–MARC tape format giving both the HEX and the display characters of each byte in the record. The first line is a guideline that numbers the bytes from 00 to 29. There are 30 bytes per per line.

The Transaction Type Code

In row 1, column 22 in Figure 10 the hex value is "02." An "02" is the code for an update transaction. Since update transactions do not result in cards being printed, you do not get any feedback for problems that may exist on the record. For example, spelling errors cannot be caught in filing and missing call numbers do not get zc cards. Most update transactions are made for retrospective conversion purposes. It is extremely important that your project definition include your anticipated needs for the OCLC–MARC data and that you develop standards and procedures to insure that the records contain all of the pertinent data.

One library entered into a retrospective conversion project with great enthusiasm but made adding their holding code to the OCLC database record their primary objective. Only after trying to use their records for a COM catalog did they realize that they had not verified that the call number on their shelflist card matched the call number on the record or that the record contained any call number at all. Conversely there are cases where items which should have been unclassified had no "x" suppression recorded, therefore it had to be assumed that the call number left in the record was valid.

Weigh the shortcuts you take in data conversion against the problems you may be creating. And always remember that what you put in is what you get out.

The transaction code is limited in the information it provides. It does not tell you that you were correcting bibliographic data or ordering new cards for a new location or adding holdings data. It provides only general information which cannot always be interpreted.

For example, all update transactions have the same code whether done using a regular or retrospective conversion authorization number, therefore you have no method of evaluating updates as to whether they are more or less important than a produce transaction on the same OCLC number. The example in Figure 9 contains an 035 field which was input to identify that this record was a recon transaction. Use of 035, 910, or 949 fields for this purpose is valid, although there is no guarantee that a commercial vendor could or would use it in processing your records.

If you develop some method of recording transaction processing codes, be sure to establish usage standards and to follow them consistently or else the integrity of your coding may be so poor that it is useless.

REPLACE transactions should be discarded. Whenever you do a REPLACE, you should follow it with another transaction (an update or produce depending upon whether the correction being made warrants new cards) to insure that you get your own version of the record. Replaces do not contain your full 049 field, local call number (e.g., 090 if an 050 is present; 099), 590 notes, etc.

REPLACE transactions have one function, to correct the on-line database record. It is questionable as to why they appear on transaction tapes at all. If your program ignores REPLACE transactions and goes back to the record created prior to the REPLACE, then you have not benefitted from the correction to the record. You will have your local data, however.

CANCEL transactions are usually interpreted to mean that all previous transactions on that OCLC number should be discarded since a CANCEL also removes the institution's holding symbol from the OCLC database. If a CANCEL is used to eliminate copies, it would have to be followed by a PRODUCE or UPDATE to show remaining holdings at the cost of another First--Time--Use (FTU). A Serials Control Local Data Record (LDR) CANCEL does not put a transaction on the archive tape. Therefore, serials control maintenance and tape maintenance require separate actions.

Finding Fields

Returning to the sample record, to find the starting position of any field, scan the directory looking for the desired tag. Identify the starting character position of that field and add it to the base address (positions 14--16). The result pinpoints the first position of the first character of the field. The base address for this record is position 181.

Position number 36 (2nd row, column 6) begins the directory entry for the fixed field. The tag is 008, the length is 41, and starting position is 13. Add 13 to 181 to get the position number 194 (7th row, column 14). The tape version of the fixed field does not contain the mnemonics that you see on the screen display nor are the elements in the same order. In addition, OCLC mixes leader and fixed field elements together in the screen display.

All fields including the directory terminate with an end of field mark (HEX 1E) except the last which has an end of record mark (HEX 1D). Fixed fields do not contain indicators and subfield codes which is a characteristic that distinguishes them from the variable length fields.

The tags that represent the variable fields do not exist in the body of the fields. They are in the directory only, so it is only through the directory that you can determine which field the data is intended to represent.

The first variable field in the sample record is the 010 field. The tag begins in position 48 (2nd row, column 18). It has a length of 18 and starts at relative position 54. By adding 54 to 181 we derive the starting position of field 010: 235 (row 8, column 25). Notice that position 235 and 236 are blank (HEX 20). Variable fields always begin with indicators even if they are blank. Following the indicators is HEX 1F for the delimiter character which is then followed by the subfield character "a". Subfield codes are identified by the pairing of HEX 1F and a lower case alpha or, less frequently, a numeric.

The 010 field for the LCCN is a variable field, but it is created from the 001 field in the LC–MARC records so it is structured like a fixed field since positions are left for elements of the LCCN even if they are not used. The format of the 010 field is:

Position 0–2	Indicators 1 and 2
Position 3–4	Subfield code
Position 5–7	Prefix (left justified; blank filled)
Position 8–9	Date element of LCCN (2 numerics)
Position 10–15	Sequence number (6 digits; right justified; zero filled)
Position 16	Blank
Position 17+	Suffix
Position 17+	End of field mark (HEX 1E in ASCII and EBCDIC)

The hyphen is not present in the MARC format. It is supplied by the print programs for cards and screen displays. Zeros are used to pad out the sequence numbers to 6 digits in the tape format.

There are several problems in the sample record in Figures 9 and 10. Some of these are:

- A null (i.e., HEX 00) in the 010 fields. A null serves no function in an OCLC–MARC record. Its presence is an error that may have been generated in tape processing or may be on the OCLC database.

- A fill character in 050; this occurrence would not cause a problem unless the program was relying on valid data in this position.

- A fill character in the non–filing character position (i.e., indicator 2) of the 245 field. To determine whether the title begins with an article, the program would have to compare the first word of the title against a table of articles based on the language codes in the fixed field and/or the 041 field.

- Brackets in the title. Bracketed data can be difficult to use, particularly in trying to determine if it should be included or excluded from printing, sorting, and indexing.

- A questionable 300 field possibly resulting from poor quality control in retrospective conversion update. The field contains a HEX BE which is the ASCII character for the script "l" and what appears to be garbled or repeated pagination data.

Additional Processing Considerations

Any local processing of OCLC–MARC data involves acknowledging the following conditions and determining a method for resolving them:

- Use of the second indicator in the 1XX tag group to generate a subject heading card. Some systems do not use this indicator nor is it currently accepted practice. Many records have the indicator set to produce a subject card as well as having a 6XX for the same name resulting in a duplicate heading condition.

- Many 590 fields were used specifically for card–related data and may have little or no application to a COM, online, or circulation display. Sometimes usage has not been consistent, therefore not all 590 fields are applicable but determining which are difficult.

- Policies and practices in usage of 049, 500, 590, and 910 fields have changed through the years, but documentation has not been kept to enable identification of the changes.

- Many vendors assume that the four-character OCLC holding library codes have a one-to-one relationship to the location of the item and do not handle "dummy" codes, usage of multiple codes for the same location, and input stamps which sub-divide a holding code.

- A former practice of using the pronoun in series entries when the name portion was the same as the main entry can cause some problems in offline file processing. This practice adds a level of complexity to the data for COM displays and online database indexing. The problem is particularly acute when the title portion is incorrectly subfielded or the name portion should not be the entire main entry but just part of it.

- 099 and 098 call number fields take precedence over other fields in the record. This is important to convey to processors of the data or else there is a tendency to look for the profiled call number field.

- It is crucial that the processor knows what the hierarchy of call numbers is and which call number to use if there are multiple ones of the same type. OCLC uses the last occurrence for cards, but some vendors have been known to use the first.

- The use of 69X fields on serial records for subject headings derived from the LC subject heading list can cause duplicate heading conditions which may require special handling in the batch or online product. It is not an infrequent occurrence to have a 650 and a 690 containing the same text.

- Existence of local 690 and 691 fields in the tape record (particularly for recon updates) will result in these fields being on any products generated from those records since software cannot distinguish between 69X fields deliberately recorded and those simply left in the online record.

- Some vendors cannot handle special characters and diacritics. They usually purge them from the records before generating the product.

- Many programmers have never dealt with variable length fields and records. If your local computer facility is planning to process your file, make sure that adequate documentation is available, that someone from the library acts as a liaison, and that a learning curve is built into any schedule.

- Some usage of input stamps only have application in the card product. Sometimes, libraries follow different practices from item to item which makes it difficult to determine what action should be taken for any given record.

- Some vendors do not deal with indicators that determine usage decisions: i.e., 240 and 6XX fields.

- Use of abbreviations in headings (e.g., Soc. condit.) which could be accommodated in a manual filing system, are less acceptable in a batch or online system. The only solution is to have a conversion table to attempt to spell out all known abbreviations. Such a table would be quite large since many variations have been used.

- Use of 500 fields for local holdings data (e.g., FOR HOLDINGS SEE MAIN ENTRY CARD) can cause problems in trying to use tape data since the information may not be applicable to another environment. It also makes the data less attractive for data sharing purposes. A possible solution is to delete all 500 fields with such data if those fields can be readily identified.

- The use of the printer port to strip off records for loading into other databases or for local processing has become a popular method of getting machine readable data. However, it should be stressed that the product of this practice is not a strict MARC record. The data is extracted in the OCLC screen display format. A MARC record is not just the content of the fields but the format of the whole record. The shareability of a record pulled from the printer port is limited, and the ability to convert it to an exact MARC record may not be available to you.

- Use of one OCLC record for multiple titles is extremely risky. Most tape processing procedures use the OCLC number as the primary value for determining a unique item. If multiple records with the same OCLC number appear on a transaction tape, it is assumed that either the last occurrence is the most up-to-date and discard all previous records, or that the holdings from all transactions should be merged into the last occurrence. In either case, bibliographic data will be lost if the previous transactions were, in fact, for different titles or editions. Again, practices that seemed feasible for getting cards produced are not at all feasible for tape processing.

- OCLC profiles for cards may not be applicable to other products. Changes made through the years may affect processing of records for such products. For example,

  - The tape file may contain records for holding library codes which may have been discontinued, but the holdings have not been deleted.

  - Discontinued codes may be reused for new locations which means reconciling old records and new records with the same four character code which has different meanings.

  - Use of multiple holding library codes for the same location in order to get different card print requirements means having to recognize that the codes do not have a one--for--one relationship with a physical location in the library and that records for multiple codes have to be combined to get the total holdings for a location.

  - Use of one holding library code for multiple locations with the use of input stamps or 099 field call numbers is a common practice. It is used primarily to reduce the number of codes with which operators must deal, but it does add some complexity to record processing.

One final topic of information. The OCLC tape documentation identifies the tape data that differs from the card or online image for that item. This data falls into two categories: data that is supplied by the card print program and data that is suppressed by the card print program. In essence, everything that is seen on the screen display appears on the tape record. This includes all subject heading fields regardless of source; 240 fields not specifically deleted; all call number fields regardless of profiled scheme; and, of course, all 049, 590, 910, and 949 field data specifically input.

The data that does not appear on the tape record is primarily that data which is supplied on the catalog cards by the card production software and the institution's profile: brackets around non-LC subject headings, media designators, and uniform titles; automatic and oversize stamps that are profile driven; profile supplied 910 data; and all print constants such as "CONTENTS:"; and ISBD space-dash-space punctuation. REPLACE transactions are a special case in that all local fields (049, 09X, 590, 910, and 949) are stipped from the record. The 049 that is retained is the default (main holding library code only).

Conclusion

Manipulating OCLC–MARC transaction tapes to generate useful products such as COM catalogs, circulation databases, online files, or even printed listings of records is a challenging process. The complexity of the record structure and the variations in standards and practices over the years make "exceptions to the rules" commonplace and "this condition should never occur" rare. The best advice I can give to a novice is:

– Become intimately familiar with the documentation for OCLC–MARC tapes and the MARC communications format.

– Document local practices in data editing and uses of local fields.

– Develop thorough specifications for the product(s) desired.

– Examine a random selection of record printouts, particularly groups of duplicates, to see what is actually in the records.

– Develop a small file of records that contain as many of the test conditions as possible and test software thoroughly!

The complexity of the format, the changes in the format and the standards for the recording of data in that format, and the variations in requirements for products generated from that data all contribute to making the development of services and systems challenging. For all of these reasons, one should enter this process with a spirit of adventure.

An Overview of Tape File Processing at SOLINET

Richard E. James
Manager, System Operations
SOLINET

The Southeastern Library Network processes MARC transactions for libraries throughout the Southeast. An overview of the procedures followed at the SOLINET Data Center in order to ensure timely and accurate processing of the files is presented. In addition, several practical suggestions for those who may be contemplating the initiation of their own in-house processing activity are offered.

This paper addresses the physical tape media, and some of the basics of tape file processing, with the idea in mind that you might be managing the tape file processing at your own institution. Also included is a brief overview of the OCLC archive tape processing performed at the SOLINET Data Center.

Physical Tape Media

First, let's examine the physical media. A standard nine inch reel of magnetic computer tape is the most popular tape used in computer centers throughout the country today. However, there is also a five inch reel of tape, often called a mini-reel. The mini-reel obviously holds less information because it is smaller. Although this tape is the same in most other respects, you should be aware that a tape drive designed for a five inch reel may not accommodate a nine inch reel. This fact can be important to you if you are acquiring a local circulation system. Some circulation vendors provide tape drives which can use only the smaller tapes. Thus, you will want to specify that your input file be delivered on the proper tape reel size.

Several other comments on compatibility may be found to be useful. In addition to considering the tape size, you should know whether your encoding scheme is ASCII or EBCDIC, and whether your recording density is 800, 1600, or 6250 characters per inch. Although nine track tape drives are the most common, the number of tracks may vary between seven or nine. While this is the most common format for the exchange of information between libraries, you should be sure that you can accommodate the format in which your information is being delivered.

On the back of each tape reel is a plastic ring that can be removed from the tape. This ring is called a write-ring, and only when it is in place can anything be written on the tape. Thus, if you have any data files on tape that you don't want to lose, you should be sure that the write-ring has been removed.

Around the outside of the tape reel is a plastic band called a Wrightline seal. When the operator loads a tape to be written on, he puts the write-ring in the back of the reel, removes the tape seal, places the tape on the hub of the drive, and then presses the appropriate load buttons. The tape drives are self-loading; that is, they thread the tape through the use of air pressure and vacuum. As a result, the operator should never have to touch the magnetic tape itself.

Two other things that are of interest about the tape reel are the label and the tape number. When the operator finishes writing the information on the output tape, a label is prepared which is stuck on the tape when it is removed from the drive. This label information is then cataloged in the directory that is maintained of all tapes in the tape library. The numbers on the tapes are analogous to the call number used on a book in that they are location devices. When a particular file is needed, the operator finds the file in the directory by the label name. He then goes into the tape library, which is organized by tape number, and retrieves the tape reel with the proper number. In many cases, a file will consist of more than one tape.

Problems in reading magnetic tape typically arise either from failing to keep the magnetic tape clean or from damage to the magnetic tape. Normally a tape cleaner is used after a tape has been passed ten times. In addition to using the tape cleaner, the operator cleans all of the tape drives at least once on each working shift. Tape can be rendered unusable if it is nicked, torn, or merely creased by a defective tape drive. Defective drives can also stretch the tape. Tape left in the back window of a car on a sunny day may also stretch due to uneven expansion as it heats up.

Tape File Processing

Next, I will briefly explain some basic procedures for processing files. If you are acquiring tape files from SOLINET, they are delivered on a tape that I'll call a "Transaction" tape. Typically, your computer center will process this tape to produce a "Master" tape in a simple process that can be diagrammed as follows:

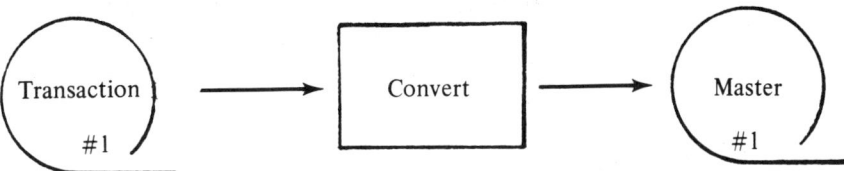

The Master tape is then used as an input file for products such as edit lists or COM catalogs. However, when the next tape file is received from SOLINET, you will want to convert it and merge it with your previous Master in such a way that you don't lose the previous Master:

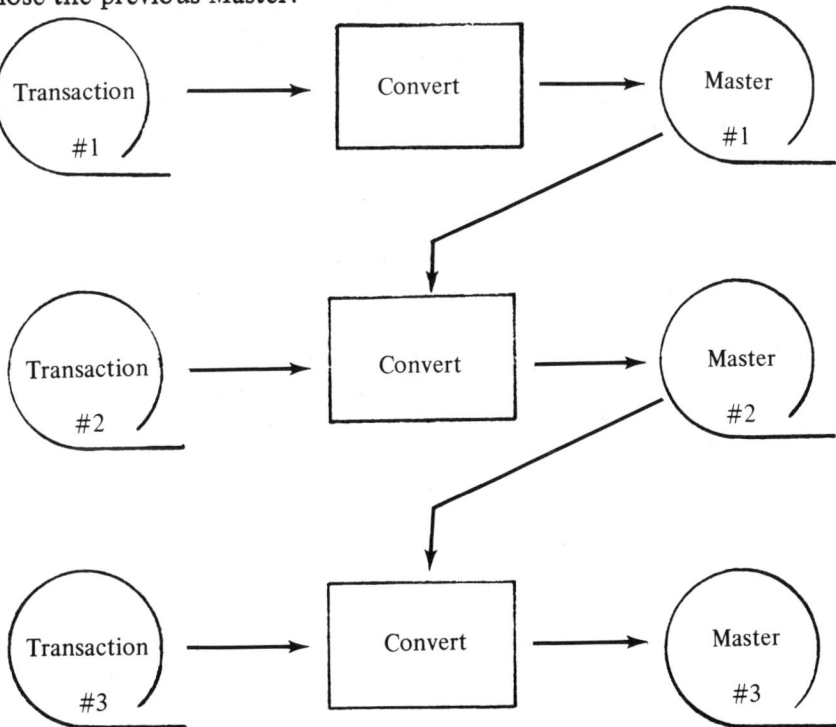

Blank tapes and tapes which may be reused are often referred to as "scratch" tapes. Each time a new transaction tape is received, you will create a new Master on a scratch tape. At the SOLINET Data Center, we maintain three generations of backup before we begin scratching data tapes. A generation of backup consists of the Master plus all of the Transaction(s) necessary to create the next Master. If you have the previous Master, but you lack the Transactions to create the current Master, you don't have backup for the current Master.

Most computer centers have backup procedures similar to the ones described. However, if your institution doesn't have a computer center, and you are operating your own local system, I would suggest that you employ tape backup procedures like these.

SOLINET Processing

At SOLINET, we are receiving MARC transactions representing all of the cataloging activity done by our membership. In addition to using the backup procedures I have described above, we edit the records to screen out corrupted data; we produce an institution summary used to update an institution profile; and we reformat the records so we can store about 40,000 records per reel instead of the usual 20,000 that the reels contain when they are delivered. The records are then sorted by institution, OCLC number, date, and sequence number.

Summary

Physical tape media and tape processing techniques have been presented. In addition, a brief overview of tape activities at SOLI-- NET has been outlined. Tape file processing offers an efficient method of storing and accessing data. If you adhere to appropriate standards, your tape file processing activities will be effective and troublefree.

Processing OCLC Tapes for COM Catalog Production:
Georgia Institute of Technology

Julia Zimmerman
Head, Systems and Data Base Management Department
Georgia Institute of Technology Library

The Georgia Tech Library has been processing MARC formatted tapes for 18 years, including LC MARC I, LC MARC II, and OCLC-MARC tapes. The data have been used mainly for production of COM catalogs. A series of programs transforms transactions from OCLC tapes to catalog records appropriate for a public catalog. The steps these programs perform are described in detail and illustrate some of the many functions OCLC tape processing must accomplish. Transaction coding using the 949 tag is also presented.

History

The Georgia Institute of Technology Library has had many years of experience in processing tapes of machine readable cataloging data. Since 1965, when the Library joined the MARC pilot project and began using MARC data for producing computer-printed catalog cards, we have been building a local bibliographic database. We joined OCLC through SOLINET in 1974 and in early 1975 began receiving our cataloging through OCLC tapes rather than LC-MARC tapes. Use of tapes for local card production was superseded by a computer output microfiche catalog in 1971, and tape processing has been directed toward COM production for the last twelve years.

Programmers at Georgia Tech had to deal with three different MARC formats during these years. The first was MARC I, followed by MARC II in 1972. Integrating the MARC I and II records was a challenge, as there were some differences significant to our program structure. In the mid-seventies when we joined OCLC, we had to make adjustments for OCLC-MARC, which is similar to LC MARC II but has some significant variations.

At that time, Georgia Tech was still maintaining a card catalog, and the OCLC-produced catalog cards had come promptly. Because few libraries were interested in acquiring archive tapes back then, it took OCLC about six months to send them to us.

At this early stage, OCLC had not prepared adequate user documentation for those who were experimenting with tapes. Our systems staff badly needed thorough information. It is typical for documentation to be the last part of a software project to be completed, so no one was surprised that when the documentation was finally available, it was lacking in some important aspects. After much perseverance and personal help from OCLC and SOLINET staff, our programmers were successful in reading the tapes. However, it was somewhat later that we acquired truly complete documentation.

The next task was figuring out how to integrate the OCLC-MARC records with the old MARC I and MARC II hybrid format. Whenever possible, the old records were changed to conform with the new, but in some cases it was more feasible to alter the OCLC-MARC record structure to match the LC–MARC records. To this day our OCLC tape processing includes steps necessitated by the merging of these three generations of MARC records.

Perhaps because the majority of OCLC users use the utility exclusively for card production, OCLC's cataloging subsystem seems to be heavily oriented toward production of catalog cards, rather than support of archival tape use. This was Tech's experience in 1975 and still seems to be the case. For example, in January 1981, OCLC made significant changes to the screen format to reflect the thousands of AACR2 entry changes made in December. Changes necessary to accommodate the new descriptive rules were also made. Subfield w's, 87X tags, altered conference entries, and other variations resulted.

Tape customers were informed of these changes at about the same time as card customers, which was a few weeks before the changes took effect for some formats, and as much as a month afterwards for other formats. We were not able to compensate for the changes without some fairly extensive program alterations; this caused considerable delay in our weekly processing. Ideally, OCLC tape users should have been given the information long before the changes were enacted in order to be prepared.

In spite of difficulties of this type, OCLC still seems to be the best source of machine readable cataloging data. We have been able to produce COM catalogs successfully using OCLC tapes for the past eight years.

The remainder of this paper concentrates on the operations performed in order to transform an OCLC archival tape into data appropriate for a COM catalog.

Programs Used to Process Tapes

OCLC tapes are received and processed weekly. A completely new catalog is produced at the beginning of each quarter, with a supplement about six weeks after each cumulative -- a total of eight catalogs a year. As weekly tapes are processed, the output is dumped into a file called the "mini-masterfile." When it is time to produce a cumulative catalog, the "mini" is dumped into the "main masterfile", which is the full bibliographic database.

Currently, Georgia Tech produces catalogs for several other University of Georgia System libraries, each of which has a different schedule for receipt of tapes and production of catalogs. The processing of tapes is essentially the same for all of us.

What operations must be performed on an OCLC tape to produce data appropriate for COM production? An overview of Georgia Tech's three main tape processing programs is useful in understanding the front end of our COM production system. These programs are called OCLC, RAWDATA, and EDIT 949. They are coordinated by one master procedure. The sequence of programs, creation and use of files, and procedural activity may be followed by referring to the flow chart (figure 1).

The master procedure, as its first step, checks to ensure that the previous week's processing was successfully completed. It then implements the first program, OCLC.

OCLC Program

(1) The program called OCLC rearranges the bibliographic records from chronological order – the order in which transactions occurred -- to OCLC control number order. By putting records in control number order, the program can spot duplicate numbers, accept the most recent occurrence, and discard the earlier versions. It rewrites the numbers into Tech ID number format, which consists of adding leading zeros to make the numbers compatible with other control numbers used in our system.

(2) The program translates the data from ASCII, a character representation code used by OCLC's computer, to that used by Tech's CDC Cyber computers, CDC Display Code. Unfortunately, this code does not easily support upper and lower case alphabetic characters and has other limitations as well. Therefore, this translation uses some rather unorthodox symbols and codes to avoid losing diacritics, uppercase letters, and certain other data elements.

(3) The OCLC program tests for certain record types by checking the appropriate fixed field elements. The records are then divided into three files:

Figure 1, Pt. 1

OCLC TAPE PROCESSING
Georgia Institute of Technology
Price Gilbert Memorial Library

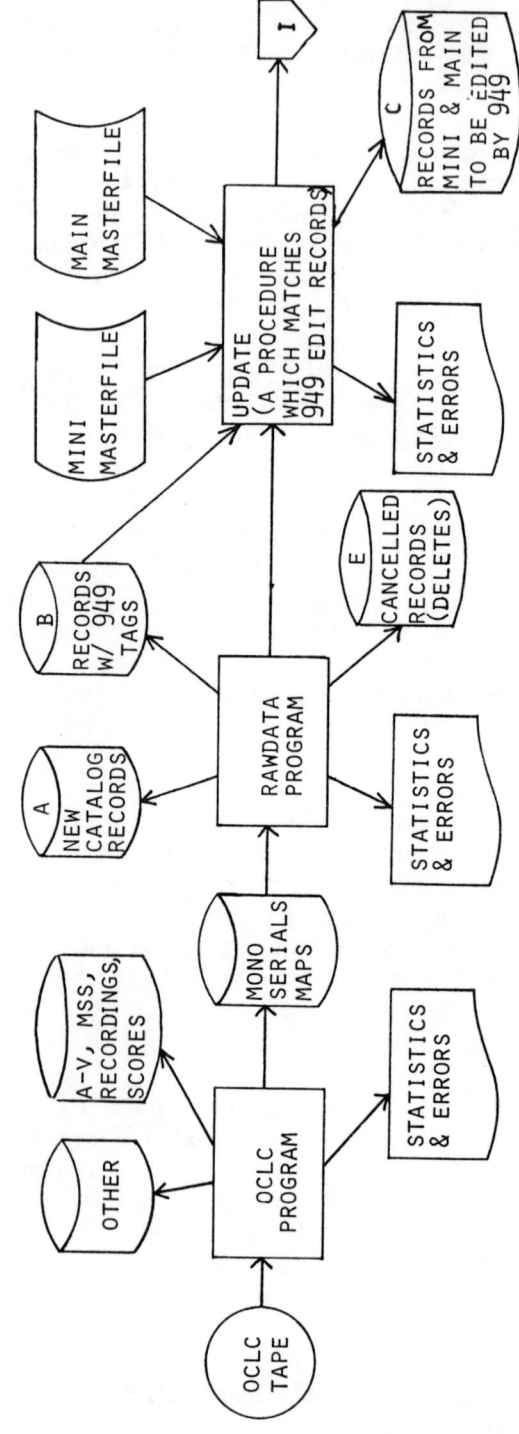

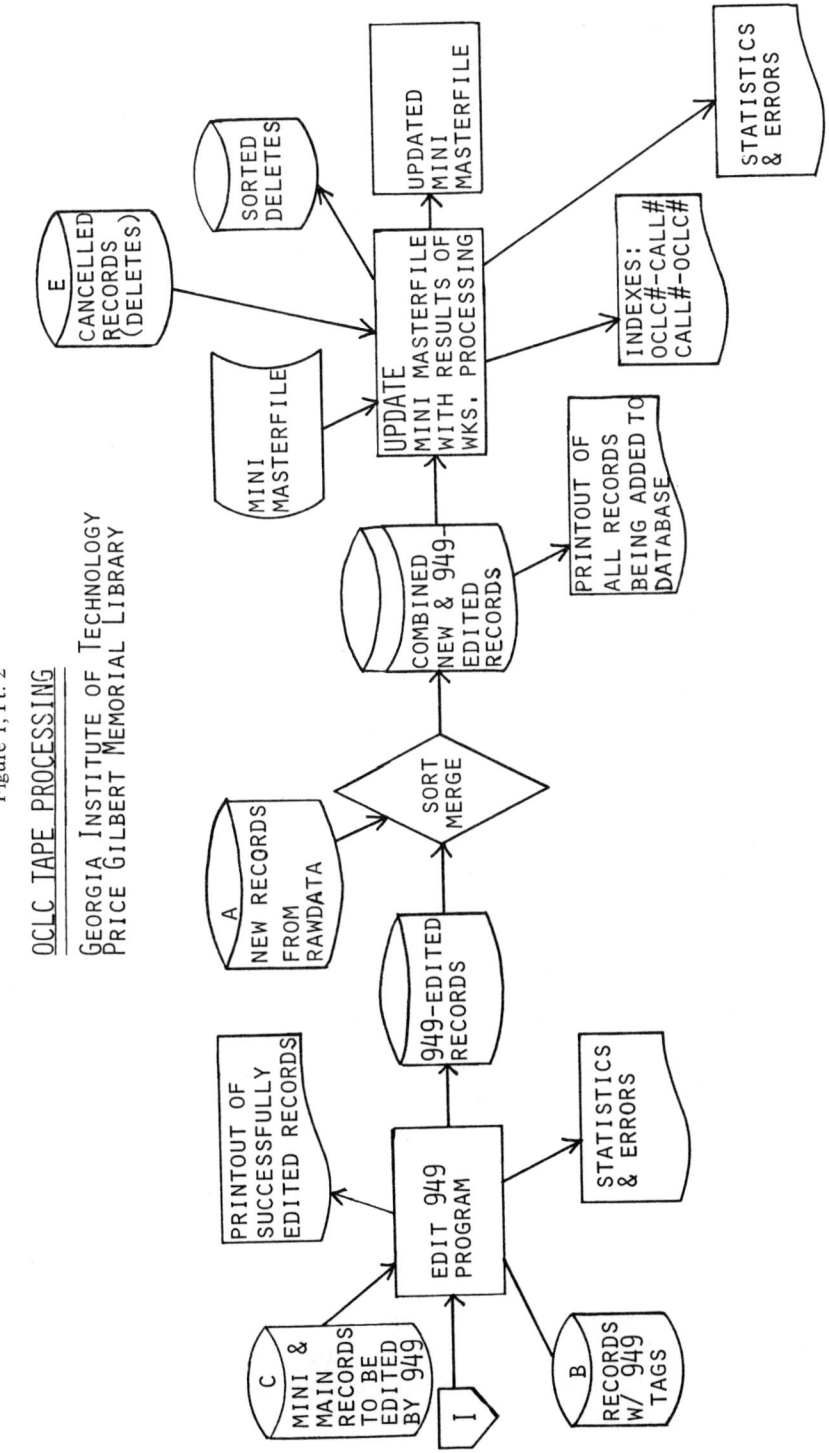

Figure 1, Pt. 2

OCLC TAPE PROCESSING

Georgia Institute of Technology
Price Gilbert Memorial Library

Monographs, Maps and Serials: this file, which contains the types of records currently in our COM catalog, becomes the working file on which the remaining programs will operate.

Audiovisuals, Recordings, Scores, and Manuscripts: these records are probably the result of error, as we do not collect or catalog these material types.

Other: a record in this file has an error in the Bibliographic Level fixed field area. This file, as well as the previous one, is printed out later so that the problems can be investigated.

At this point, the OCLC Program has finished its part in the week's processing. The master procedure retires it and initiates the second program, RAWDATA.

RAWDATA *Program*

Just as it takes sophisticated programming to process OCLC tapes, it requires considerable intellectual effort to make the decisions on which programming is based. These decisions include choosing which fields should be deleted entirely, which should be retained and printed in the finished product, and which should be stored in the database but not printed. Interpreting indicators and subfield codes, determining the order of elements in the final record, and supplying punctuation and print constants must be included in the specifications. Only knowledgeable library personnel are qualified to make such decisions.

OCLC has done the necessary programming for card production. But when a library processes tapes in-house, librarians must play an active role in examining the data and deciding how best to process it for their library's needs.

The RAWDATA program includes the programming that enacts many of these decisions. It begins by subdividing the working file (Monographs, Maps and Serials) into still more files. It also produces statistical reports and performs certain other functions which bring the new records into conformity with those already in the database.

(1) RAWDATA identifies records which have a 949 field and sorts them into a file for later processing. The 949 tag is used at Tech for partial editing of OCLC records, specifically serials records on which detailed holdings notes change frequently. The actual editing takes place later, handled by the EDIT 949 program, which will be examined in detail in the next section.

(2) RAWDATA identifies records on which the CANCEL command has been sent. It sorts these records into a special file so that they can be matched with main masterfile records, causing the latter to be deleted from the database.

(3) RAWDATA begins to revise the records which remain after cancelled and 949 records are set aside. The information in each record at this point is still roughly analogous to what was on the OCLC screen at the time the record was produced. It is somewhat more compact and a few of the elements have been moved around. Additions which automatically would print on cards, such as print constants and supplied punctuation, are still lacking.

There are about 75 fields that may come on the tape that are never used in printed records; these have not yet been deleted. In addition, tags, subfield codes, indicators, leader, and record directory must all be read and interpreted before the remaining data can be correctly processed. RAWDATA performs all these functions, reformatting the raw record to a more human--readable form.

(4) RAWDATA chooses the correct call number and formats it properly. The program includes several tests to determine whether to use the 090, 050, or 086 field as the correct call number; other call number fields such as the 082 and 099 have already been discarded. Punctuation and subfield coding in the selected records' call numbers are checked. If errors are discovered, the record is placed in the growing error file to be printed out later.

(5) RAWDATA also checks to make sure that all filing indicator positions are filled. Those who have COM catalogs know that missing and incorrect filing indicators can be a major problem. Like other offending records, those with missing filing indicators are pulled into an error file.

(6) RAWDATA translates the holdings symbols in the 049 field into a one--character location code, which is stored in the fixed field of the local record. The structure of the fixed field in our database is similar to OCLC's fixed field. It is permanently retained as part of each record, although it is not printed in the COM catalog.

(7) RAWDATA's final chore is to produce statistics on the number of records processed, the frequency and types of errors, as well as lists of updated, produced, and cancelled transactions.

As mentioned before, it also prints out copies of problem records to aid in the correction of errors.

EDIT 949 Program

The third program, which completes weekly processing, is EDIT 949. In a database created and maintained through OCLC, an "update" transaction sends an entirely new record to replace the old record. Sometimes this method is efficient. However, when the record in the local database is substantially different from the OCLC record, updating is time-consuming as it often requires re-keying of a large portion of the record. Because of the frequent updates needed to maintain serials holdings notes, we decided several years ago to investigate other options.

At about this same time, OCLC agreed that the 949 tag was allowable for use in transaction coding. Programmers at Tech developed a system of partial editing in which editing commands could be entered in the 949 field and directed at some portion of the record as it exists in our database.

Briefly, this is how it works. Assume that there is a record in our database which has an error. The cataloger accesses the OCLC record and checks to make sure that it has the same OCLC number as the record in our database needing correction. On the OCLC screen, the cataloger enters a 949 field which includes one or more editing "commands." The command addresses Tech's database record, not the screen record. The cataloger UPDATEs and the entire transaction comes on the weekly tape.

(1) After our OCLC program pulls all records with 949 fields into a file, the EDIT 949 program will process the edit command. It does so by using the OCLC control number to locate the record in our database needing changes, and applies the command in the 949 field to change the targeted area of our database record.

(2) The rest of the OCLC record, which served merely as a vehicle to deliver the 949 command, is deleted.

(3) After the changes or corrections have been made, EDIT 949 generates statistics on its activities and prints our copies of the records which have been changed. The procedure then retires EDIT 949, and merges all the new records from RAWDATA and the edited old ones from 949 into the mini–masterfile, signaling the end of weekly processing.

```
001537659   12017328   A   8012018012120SAL P      D OENK 18641926   U ENG
050   <ANA1 .B7
245 00<A^BUILDING NEWS AND ENGINEERING JOURNAL.
260 01<A^LONDON, B^PUBLISHED FOP THE PROPRIETORS.
300    <A 120 V.<BILL.<C30-32 CM.
362 0  <AV. 11-130; ^JAN. 1864-^MAR. 1926.
590    <A^LIBRARY HAS: V.24--25, 1873; V.29--31, 1875--1876.
690 0<A^ARCHITECTURE<X^PERIODICALS.
690 0<A^BUILDING<X^PERIODICALS.
780 00<T^BUILDING NEWS AND ARCHITECTURAL REVIEW.
785 07<T^ARCHITECT.
785 07<T^ARCHITECT AND BUILDING NEWS.
```

Figure 2. Ga. Tech database record*

---

* Less-than signs (⟨) are symbols used in Ga. Tech processing to indicate subfield codes. Circumflexes (∧) indicate capital letters.

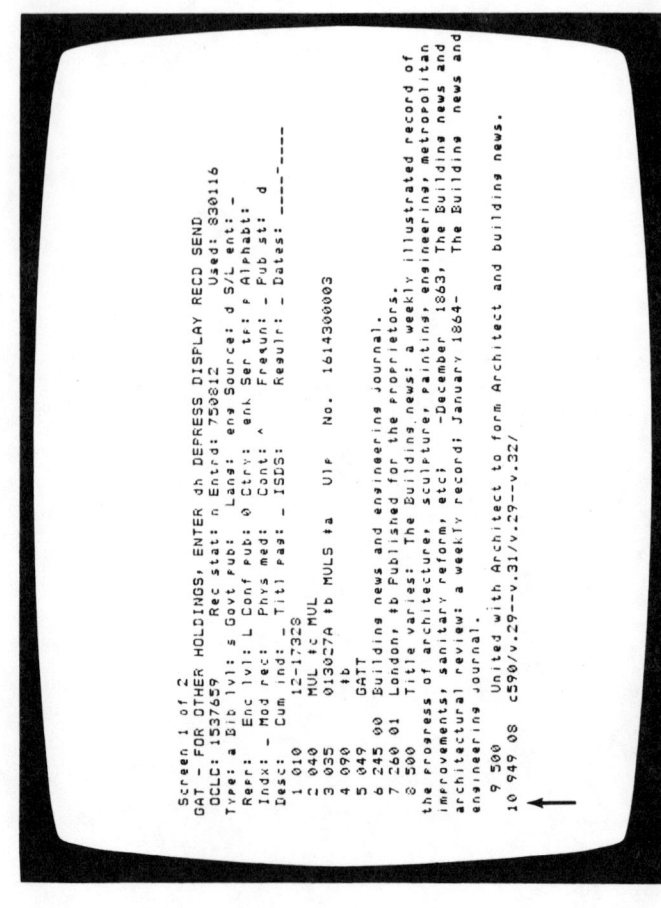

Figure 3. The "matching" OCLC record with 949 field containing a *change* command. The command tells the program to change the portion of the 590 field which reads *v. 29–31* to read *v. 29-32*.

```
001537659  12017328  A   8012918012120SAL P      D OENK 1841926   U ENG
050    <ANA1.B7
245 00<A^BUILDING NEWS AND ENGINEERING JOURNAL.
260 01<A^LONDON, B^PUBLISHED FOR THE PROPRIETORS.
300    <A 120 V.<BILL.<C30-32 CM.
362 0  <AV. 11-130; ^JAN. 1864-^MAR. 1926.
590    <A^LIBRARY HAS: V.24--25, 1873; V.29--32, 1875--1876.
690 0<A^ARCHITECTURE<X^PERIODICALS.
690 0<A^BUILDING<X^PERIODICALS.
780 00<T^BUILDING NEWS AND ARCHITECTURAL REVIEW.
785 07<T^ARCHITECT.
785 07<T^ARCHITECT AND BUILDING NEWS.
```

Figure 4. Ga. Tech database record after 949 command has been processed

CALL NUMBER: NA1 .B7   ARCHITECTURE
BUILDING NEWS AND ENGINEERING JOURNAL. V. 11-130; JAN. 1864-MAR. 1926.
  LONDON, PUBLISHED FOR THE PROPRIETORS. 120 V. ILL. 30-32 CM.
  CONTINUES: BUILDING NEWS AND ARCHITECTURAL REVIEW. MERGED WITH:
  ARCHITECT TO FORM: ARCHITECT AND BUILDING NEWS.
    T. S:ARCHITECTURE--PERIODICALS. S:BUILDING--PERIODICALS.
                                                      OCLC NO. 001537659

LIBRARY HAS:
V.24--25, 1873
V.29--32, 1875--1876

Figure 5. Ga. Tech record as it appears in the COM catalog

EDIT 949 is a complete system of editing records from archive tapes. Not only does it facilitate corrections, but it may be used to add or delete fields from records, delete records from the database, add cross references to the COM catalog, and more. (See figures 2--5 for sample records of the 949 editing system)

COM Catalog Programs

When it is time to produce a new COM catalog, there is another series of programs which operate on the mini-masterfile. In brief, the records in the mini-masterfile are sorted and formatted into the standard COM catalog format. The mini file is then merged with the main file.

The records must then be sorted together and the correct form of a record must be selected if multiples exist. There are "entry" programs which identify main and added entries, append chosen headings to the now several versions of each record, and interfile them. In this manner Author/Title, Subject, and Call Number files are created.

The sorted files are output to tape and sent to a COM vendor, who is usually required to produce our new COM catalog within a week. New OCLC tapes arrive at the Tech Library, and the entire process begins again.

It should be stressed that we do not endorse in-house tape processing for COM over the excellent COM catalog services available from commercial vendors. An understanding of the many processes which must be performed in order to make use of the data on archive tapes is important, however. Libraries can benefit from being able to assess the limitations, as well as the many exciting possibilities, afforded by the use of OCLC tapes.

Processing OCLC Tapes:
Triangle Research Libraries Network

Jeanne Sawyer
Library Systems Analyst
Triangle Research Libraries Network

The Triangle Research Libraries Network is a cooperative project of Duke University, North Carolina State University at Raleigh, and the University of North Carolina at Chapel Hill to develop a distributed network of the online catalogs of the three participating institutions. The archive tape processing system described uses tapes received through the OCLC-- MARC Subscription Service. A master database of bibliographic records for each institution, the basis for that institution's online catalog, is created and maintained.

Background

TRLN, or Triangle Research Libraries Network, is a cooperative project of the libraries at the University of North Carolina-Chapel Hill, North Carolina State University at Raleigh and Duke University in Durham. The libraries' combined collections of over six million volumes are available to meet the demands of users from the university communities and from the private and governmental research institutes in Research Triangle Park.

Use of the collections as a combined resource is greatly hampered by the difficulty of using separate card catalogs to obtain bibliographic information about materials in the collections. It is to meet this need for mutual access as well as to provide the more efficient and flexible searching mechanisms of online information retrieval systems that the three libraries have undertaken the development of a distributed library network.

The distributed network approach is quite different from the centralized system approach taken in other online catalog development efforts. This has a profound effect on all aspects of system design, including the way archive tapes are processed. Each of the three libraries will have its own computer installation supporting its online catalog.

They will be linked using telecommunications facilities so that users with access to any one of the catalogs can have queries transmitted automatically to any or all of the other catalogs in the network. Each library maintains only its own database – there is no jointly maintained union database. The affect of this on tape processing will be discussed later.

Thus, TRLN is a cooperative project to develop a network composed of individual institution's online catalogs, each capable of handling search requests and responses from other catalogs in addition to all the usual functions of an online catalog. Actually, "online catalog" is an understatement: the systems operating at each institution will in fact be complete library systems including such functions as acquisitions, serials control and circulation. Users, regardless of their physical location, will be able to determine not only does one of the libraries own an item but whether it is on the shelf, on order, etc. To reflect this larger range of capabilities, we make an effort to refer to the system as the "Bibliographic Information System" but often simply call it the "online catalog."

TRLN Archive Tape Processing System

Before bibliographic information can be provided online, the information must be in a coherent database of machine readable records. For this reason, arranging for database creation and maintenance facilities was the first project for TRLN. In fact, all three libraries were members of SOLINET and were already creating bibliographic records in machine readable form (and to some extent maintaining them) through OCLC. This would clearly continue to be the method of choice for acquiring basic bibliographic records in machine readable form, which by definition meant archive tape processing.

On the surface, the TRLN archive tape processing system is about like any other tape processing system for OCLC archive tapes. As you know, the basic process of creating a master database from the archive tapes is quite straightforward: since archive records appear on the tape in order of record use, and since normally the most recently used record is complete and correct, creating the master record is simply a matter of finding and keeping the most recent record. Usually this is done by first eliminating "extra" records from the archive tape, thus creating a transaction file that contains only one version of each record that was used during that tape period.

This transaction file is than compared to the local master file, one record at a time. If the record is not already in the master, the archive record represents a new item and is added to the master file. If there is already a master record, then the archive record is an update and completely replaces the old master record. This is the primary task that must be accomplished by any archive tape processing system. Please note that this is an oversimplification of the basic process because there are complicated situations that must be accounted for such as handling "Replace" records and records that have been bumped in the OCLC database.

However, an archive tape processing system can do much more than just basic record manipulation, and for the TRLN libraries, some additional features were required. It is because of these additional requirements that TRLN decided to develop its own tape processing system rather than either use a vendor's system or purchase software.

Before these special features of the TRLN system are discussed, the effect the distributed approach to online catalogs has on the tape processing system should be explained. The major effect is to simplify the tape processing requirements.

Since each institution will have its own database, the TRLN system processes the tapes from only one institution at a time. It is generalized to handle differences among the three institutions, but it does not have to recognize and somehow merge records from different institutions that represent the same item. To accomplish this type of merging requires extremely close coordination of cataloging policies and practices as well as sophisticated matching programs to account for the possibility that the institutions might have used different records for the same item. You can't depend on matching record identification numbers because of duplicate records in OCLC.

The TRLN philosophy requires that, although the three libraries are similar in many respects, each has individual policies and practices that must be accommodated by the system. The libraries adopt uniform practices to the extent possible, but the individual library has the ultimate right to determine when it can accept a uniform policy and when a local policy is necessary. Thus, the requirement is compatibility, not necessarily complete uniformity. The archive tape processing system was designed to allow this flexibility. In fact, however, very few areas of conflicting policies were found and these few were resolved with little difficulty.

Special Features
   Transaction Coding

As mentioned before, the TRLN system addresses several problems in addition to the basic process of selecting the master records. As everyone who has tried to update their local machine readable records through OCLC knows, one of the biggest problems is the requirement that the entire OCLC record be re-edited in order to make any change to the local master record. This process of re-editing records is difficult and time-consuming because the local data must be reconstructed.

Since the bibliographic record that appears printed on the cards does not include all the data in the machine readable record, the cataloger cannot even see the complete record as it was originally created. The re-editing ends up being done on the basis of partial information available on the card and from memory. The whole process is very slow and requires highly trained staff even to correct simple typographical errors.

It is this condition that prompted the claim that the machine readable records were only being maintained "to some extent" through the OCLC system. Because changes are so time consuming to make, in many cases the changes were made manually in the card files, but were simply never made in the machine readable records.

Of course, the best solution to this problem is an online editing system that will allow local master records to be corrected directly. TRLN has developed such a system, which has been implemented in the TRLN libraries, but before this system was established we believed that a simpler system that could be used until the online editing system was available would be worthwhile. Therefore, a system of local transaction codes was developed that allows bibliographic data to be treated separately from holdings data.

The system developed requires that each type of data be considered in its entirety. That is, if a change to any bibliographic data element is required, all bibliographic fields must be re-edited. This is still a substantial amount of work, but we considered a more sophisticated batch system to be impractical because a) it would probably be too complicated to use and, b) the transaction code system would ultimately be replaced by the online system. The goal of the transaction code system was to provide some relief to those cataloging staff responsible for maintaining the databases as promptly but inexpensively as possible.

The transaction code system works as follows: the cataloger enters a mnemonic code into a local use field when editing an OCLC record. These codes are interpreted by the tape processing system to produce a specific action. The codes are only used to change a record that already exists in the local master database, so new records are recognized and added to the master database in the usual way.

When a transaction code appears in the archive record, the tape processing system finds the matching master record and, according to the code, instead of replacing the entire record by the new version, replaces only the bibliographic or only the holdings data. This allows cataloging staff to update holdings without reconstructing the bibliographic record or to change bibliographic data without reconstructing the holdings statement.

This system of transaction codes has worked very well for us, but a word of warning is in order for anyone considering a similar system. Using the codes means that the records on the archive tapes no longer meet the assumption of most tape processing systems that the most recent record on the tape is complete. In other words, no one should adopt such a system without absolute assurance that a tape processing system will be available that can interpret the codes.

Validation

The TRLN tape processing system also helps with the problem of detecting errors in the records. Although proof-reading is the only method for detecting errors in the actual data, automated methods can be used to detect some tagging and coding errors. Indeed, that is the only practical way to catch errors in the non-printing portions of the record.

Adequate error detection in these areas is especially important because accurate use of the records by automated systems such as online catalogs or even COM catalogs depends on the accuracy of data in the non-printing portions of the record. Many problems result not only from ordinary mistakes but also from changes in the MARC format over the years. For example, many fields now require filing indicators that have not required them in the past. This process of checking for errors is called validation, and the TRLN tape processing system does a rather extensive job of it.

In addition to checking for errors such as records with no title or no call number, the system makes cross checks between fields. For example, the system ensures that a record with a title coded as a main entry does not also have an author coded as a main entry. When the system detects an error, the complete local record, tags and all, is printed for cataloging staff to use in making the correction. We have found that although the OCLC system does some of this type of checking, there are many conditions that we regard as errors that are not checked.

It is very surprising to find that this type of extensive validation seems to be an unusual feature of tape processing systems. Given the complexity of the MARC records, the changes in the formats over time, and human nature together with the characteristics of computer processing, it seemed obvious to us that validation was a necessary feature of the tape processing system.

Error Correction

The TRLN system also corrects certain errors automatically if the appropriate correction can be determined with reasonable certainty. This feature is used primarily to supply missing filing indicators. The indicators are supplied based on the fixed field language code and a table of the language codes, initial articles and filing indicator values. These corrections are not foolproof and therefore are reviewed manually, but the review takes much less time than making the corrections manually would. The system cannot correct or even detect incorrect filing indicators, so this feature is used for mopping up and does not free the catalogers of the responsibility for filling in the indicators carefully.

Statistics Collecting

Another feature that the TRLN system does not have at present, but is planned as an enhancement, is the ability to monitor collection growth and cataloging activity based on statistics gathered by the archive tape processing system. Collection growth statistics include, for example, the number of titles and physical volumes in the library as a whole as well as within departmental libraries. Breakdowns can be maintained for each copy as to whether it was new to the institution, new to the department or an added copy at a location that already had a copy.

Cataloging activity statistics include keeping track of the source of cataloging copy (the Library of Congress, other OCLC members or the local library), the type of cataloging being done (new items, recataloging items already in the collection, etc.) and the production and type of cataloging done by individual catalogers. These statistics are all maintained manually now, and the effort is tedious, cumbersome and probably inaccurate.

Since incoming archive records, when compared to previously existing local master records, include most of the data necessary to collect these statistics, an archive tape processing system can relieve much of the burden of collecting statistics. Of course, this concept can be extended to monitor collection development as well by maintaining statistics on numbers of items added in various subject areas, language groups and the like.

Summary

Although most of this presentation has been rather specifically about the TRLN tape processing system, basic concepts about archive tape processing have been stressed. Probably the most difficult concept and also the most important for library staff, is learning to think of the machine readable master record as the library's authoritative record for that item. This requires over--coming a long--standing, gut--level conviction that the shelflist or main entry card is the master record. Until this shift in thinking is made, the machine readable record will not be taken seriously enough and the records will not be maintained properly. The cards are important, too, at least for now, but they must be re--garded as simply images of the master records rather than as the master records themselves.

Thus, the archive tape processing system becomes a tool in the catalog maintenance process, and a well--designed system can provide many aids for this process above and beyond simply selecting the most recently created version of the record. Examples include those mentioned earlier: record validation for errors, correction of certain types of errors, statistics collection and, in some cases, transaction coding to limit record editing through OCLC.

COM Catalog Problems and Solutions: Georgia State University

Christina Landram
Head, Catalog Department
Georgia State University

The development of a COM catalog is discussed beginning with the reasons for changing from a card to a COM catalog. Production of the catalog from initial contact with vendors to acceptance at the university is described.

The process of COM catalog development at Georgia State University started in the spring of 1978 when we began our first discussions as to how we would accommodate AACR 2. Would we try to incorporate new AACR 2 headings in our current card catalog? Would we begin a new catalog? If we began a new catalog, what form should it take – card, book or COM?

It seemed that if we created a new catalog, COM should certainly be considered, since we would be able to disperse the catalog to other floors in the library and to other locations on campus and off campus. A COM catalog would also provide us with an opportunity to look at our machine readable file and to clean up that file in preparation for an online catalog.

Discussions were begun with our Georgia State Computer Center regarding production of a COM catalog; and, beginning in the fall of 1978 meetings were held on a monthly basis. If a catalog could be developed locally, it seemed that more control could be maintained regarding the end product. A sample MARC tape was acquired so that the Computer Center could become familiar with the format.

Our sister institution, Georgia Institute of Technology, had had a COM catalog for some years, and we talked with them about the possibility of using their programs. They kindly consented to furnish us with a set of their programs. However, their hardware and ours were not compatible. Their computer operated in 6 bits and ours in 8 bits and therefore we could not use the actual programs, although we could have used only the logic from them.

Our plan was to begin the new catalog using only those items cataloged after January 1981 when AACR 2 was scheduled to go into effect. Personnel at the Computer Center, who are also library patrons, could not understand why we did not use all our machine readable records. They aptly pointed out that patrons would not be likely to use a COM catalog which consisted of only one fiche. Their point was well taken, and we began to look at the situation from the standpoint of using all our machine readable records, which went back to 1975.

If we used in the same catalog AACR 2 headings and pre-AACR 2 headings, then we felt that we needed automated authority control, so that the earlier headings could be converted automatically. But automated authority control is a very complex process. Our computer center estimated that to develop the system we wanted we would spend approximately $250,000 in development costs alone. Because the figure was so high, the GSU Computer Center recommended that we use an outside vendor.

Search for Outside Vendor

Early in 1979 we developed specifications to be sent to all known vendors asking them if they could supply a product which met these specifications. We identified the formats and tags which we needed to have included. One of the very important ones was the ability to print the print constants used in the serial format.

We were also interested in how the catalog would sort and we specified the preferred filing rules -- those used in a publication by John Rather entitled *Filing Arrangement in the Library of Congress Catalogs*, published in 1971. These were the only library filing rules with which we were acquainted which considered the use of a computer in arranging a library catalog. The current publication entitled *Library of Congress Filing Rules*, 1980, is based on this earlier publication.

One question we forgot to ask was "on how many characters do you sort?" In the card catalog we looked at as many characters as necessary in order to file the card. Computers, however, like to be told when they have reached an end and so sorting is done on a finite number. If the sort was on 20 characters rather than 100, obviously very long headings would sort at random. We did ask a vendor if it had automated subject authority control. We knew of one who had automated name authority control at that time so we asked if this was under development.

Another very important item which we requested in the specifications was a product to be received with each catalog which was called a "master file." This was done at the request of our computer center and we are indebted to them for suggesting this. The master file is defined as: "With each catalog, in machine readable form a current copy of each bibliographical record for each title that is the result of all authority control, local changes and corrections in the OCLC format and arranged in OCLC number order."

We encountered some difficulty in getting the information we needed from vendors. Also, some vendors provided some of the items but not others. A table was drawn up listing our needs and what items each vendor could supply. On the basis of these needs and what vendors supplied, a vendor was chosen. The records were shipped August 5, 1980 with our first catalog due December 1, 1980.

Unfortunately, the relationship with the vendor did not progress to our satisfaction. We received our catalog sixteen weeks late. When it arrived we discovered that it had no holding library symbols. That is, you could not tell if a title was in the general collection, the reference collection, a newspaper, etc. This made the catalog unusable for any purpose.

We immediately chose another vendor and this second vendor operated through a "middleman." The "middleman" performed some of the operations and the vendor other operations. This shared responsibility had its advantages and disadvantages.

In the beginning it was an advantageous arrangement because the "middleman" helped us to understand the limitations of the COM product. However, going through a third party to get answers to questions is not as effective as going to the vendor directly.

Our first catalog was received in June 1981. We also ordered a classed catalog but the first edition we received had no holding library symbols. The second edition of the classed catalog had holding library symbols but did not include any call numbers which we had input into the 099 field. Because of these communication and procedural difficulties we are now operating directly with the COM vendor.

The 8th edition of our catalog has now been received. This edition was sorted by the new *ALA Filing Rules*, which were published in 1980, and, of course, were written from the standpoint of sorting by a computer.

Costs of COM Production

Costs from COM vendors vary greatly. This is due primarily to the fact that vendors offer different services. Before we chose our first vendor, we created a table listing the kinds of services vendors supplied. We elected to abandon the classed catalog, principally because of cost. It increased the cost of our catalog by about 40 per cent. We now receive three editions of the catalog per year. Each edition is a cumulative one. Our latest edition, which included 186,206 titles, cost slightly over $17,000.

Each edition consists of a general catalog in two parts: subject and author/title. Formerly we received in fiche, as a subset of this catalog, a separate serials catalog, which was also composed of a subject and an author/title catalog. But this had to be dropped due to its high cost. We now receive a hard copy list of periodicals with holdings and limited tags printed. To supplement it we maintain an in--house serials edit list produced on fiche from the master file. It shows all serial records in the MARC format and is sorted by call number.

We do not receive any supplements. In place of supplements we have an in--house COM product produced weekly through GSU Computer Center which is called an *In Process File*. It is updated weekly and lists in main entry and title arrangements items on standing order, items ordered, those in cataloging, those at the bindery and those which have been completed. Completed items and standing order items have the call number input into the record. All items cataloged, other than standing order items, automatically drop off the *In Process File* after 360 days. This gives us an overlap with the COM. Due to the automatic drop off procedure, we do not have to manually weed the file.

The acceptance of our COM catalog by faculty and students at GSU has been rewarding to us. The favorable response to it may have been helped by the fact that so many of our students work and encounter fiche and film in their jobs. Also, Atlanta Public Library has a catalog on film. We did undertake a public relations program with articles in the university newspaper and signs in the library. And we tried to involve staff in all aspects of it very early. When the catalog was first received we staffed a special desk to assist patrons in its use.

There was some skepticism on part of the staff and as a result we continued to receive cards for an add--on catalog for some months longer than necessary. In the summer of 1983 some members of the Catalog Department surveyed patrons' use of the COM and card catalogs. Of 648 usable questionnaires, 63.2% found the COM easier to use and 65% found it faster to use.

Use and Improvement

Have we succeeded in our original goals? Well, we have increased our original 25 copies ordered to 51 and if we counted the superseded editions we send out, we would add another 36 to that 51.

Have we cleaned up our file? That concern is addressed in

another paper in this volume. What about authority control for names? In June 1983 automated authority control was run against our catalog for the first time. As with most new programs there were problems. Almost all these had been cleared up by October 1983, so that our goal of AACR 2 conversion had been attained.

As far as any advice I might give librarians who are considering acquiring COM catalogs, my first maxim is "Don't expect it to be a perfect product." It is an evolving product and items which could be improved in a first edition, may be improved in the second, but something else may occur which needs to be changed. My second bit of advice I might offer is that it might be helpful to anticipate skepticism from some of the staff and be prepared to deal with that situation.

Implementation of a CLSI Circulation System: Winthrop College

Laurance R. Mitlin
Assistant Dean of Library Services
Winthrop College

Winthrop College took delivery of a CLSI circulation system in 1981. The decisions made and the problems faced in loading bibliographic data from the library's archival tapes are detailed. Factors to be considered are listed, and advice to potential tape users is given.

Background

At Winthrop College, a CLSI circulation system was installed in 1981 with plans to load the bibliographic data from our OCLC–MARC archival tapes. The tape load was completed in the middle of February, 1982.

Our experience in this process should be valuable to anyone contemplating the implementation of a circulation system. Since our database has been loaded for eighteen months, we have had time to discover most of the probable anomalies that exist in the file.

Loading data from MARC tapes on a CLSI system requires a good deal of planning in the current version of the system. There are two reasons for this: (1) CLSI will not load a MARC record without reformatting -- unless an optional tape load module is purchased, and (2) the system has great flexibility as to how data is stored.

While a MARC record has virtually no limits on the number of data fields allowed, CLSI will only permit thirty variable fields. So a priority list of data – in a library's perception of the field's importance – must be developed. While it is likely that the overwhelming majority of cataloging records will fit comfortably in thirty fields, there will be some that will have too many notes, subjects, or other fields.

After many painful concessions by the cataloging department, we settled on twenty-eight fields. We did not use all thirty fields on the advice of CLSI -- advice I'm not sure was appropriate and advice they no longer give.

Next we had to decide which MARC fields would transfer to which CLSI fields. The OCLC publication, *OCLC–MARC Subscription Service Documentation,*[1] was invaluable in this task as it discusses all possible fields in all formats. The most difficult decisions here were with the many notes pertaining to serials.

The intent of our decisions was to store sufficient information to institute an online catalog at some future time. Not surprisingly, the term "sufficient" was subject to different definitions by library staff. Unfortunately, when we added up the storage space required to hold our records in this form, we found we could not afford to buy the disk storage necessary. So we fell back to a minimal record for circulation purposes. Thus, our first lesson learned was that the amount of storage space needed to store MARC records is very large.

Although complete records of our retrospective cataloging could not be stored, we did program our OCLC--CLSI online interface with the original twenty-eight fields for current cataloging. This has given us some experience with our decisions.

Converting MARC to CLSI

The impracticality of one seemingly "good idea" became obvious very quickly. We thought displaying added authors and titles next to the main authors and titles would be logical and helpful to the patron. We saw no need to reproduce an old-fashioned catalog card on a CRT screen. Unfortunately, a MARC record is more of a catalog card reproduction than we thought. Because punctuation, especially brackets, can extend from the 245 field through the description, edition, and imprint statements, some strange looking displays result when added entries are inserted in the middle of bracketed information. With the advent of International Standard Bibliographic Description (ISBD), the problem no longer exists as brackets must be closed within a field. Unfortunately, the earlier cataloging almost forces you to stick with a traditional card format unless you are willing to overlook brackets.

Another problem is caused by the 512 character limit in CLSI fields, about half as many as are allowed in a MARC field. We have had an occasional note truncated because of this. The OCLC-CLSI online interface conveniently places an ellipsis at the point of truncation. This situation was overcome by splitting a lengthy note into two successive fields.

---

[1] Online Computer Library Center. *OCLC--MARC Subscription Service Documentation.* 4th ed. Dublin, OH, 1981.

SOLINET Conversion

SOLINET, following our reformatting specifications as shown in figure 1, processed our archival tape records and created tapes to be loaded on our CLSI system. In addition to reformatting, SOLINET also derived the "author–title key," CLSI's equivalent of an OCLC number, from the 1XX and 245 fields. If we had desired, SOLINET also would have created copy or "item–level" records and assigned statistical category codes.

The SOLINET conversion program handles most potential problems. OCLC–MARC supports a character set that is much larger than the standard computer terminal can handle. The SOLINET program converts non–standard characters, such as AE, cursive l (el), etc., to the nearest standard equivalent.

One potentially serious deficiency in the SOLINET program is its inability to provide print constants. All elements that appear on an OCLC printed card are not present on the CRT screen or on the archival tape. These elements are provided by the print program, based on the library's profile and on the indicators that precede each field. Most introductory phrases in "notes" fields, for example, are determined by indicators. If the tape conversion program does not supply print constants, the reformatted records will not have initial phrases like: "Contents", "Continues", "Continued by", etc.

The SOLINET program will provide automatic stamps, and only one manual (input) stamp. It may be either the one above or the one below the call number on a catalog card. It cannot be both. This may be a problem, depending upon a library's practices.

Figure 1
Reformatting Specifications

CLSI Tag Number	MARC Tags
01	CAL,$ (Call number, spaces deleted)
02	Automatic stamp and Input stamp above call number
03	100;110;111
04	130;240
05	245
.	
.	
.	
28	001, bytes 4-10 (OCLC number)

Record Problems

Considering that 175,000 records have been loaded, the number of problems with the data on those records is relatively small. A list of some of the problems experienced should prove instructive.

The author--title key is derived from the 1XX and 245 fields. If the second indicator is wrong in the 245 field, the conversion program or the interface will consider an article as a significant word and derive an incorrect key.

CLSI will index any field desired, limited only by the storage space available to store the indexes. The indexing program is designed to ignore initial articles, so an incorrect indicator will not interfere with proper retrieval. However, an old cataloging practice, no longer followed, will cause problems. This was the practice of preceding titles with an ellipsis when anything on the title page was omitted.

The computer expects the ellipsis to be supplied when a title search is done. While the number of such titles is very small, the ellipses should be deleted whenever such a record is used. CLSI will ignore punctuation *within* a field, though. This limits the negative effects some authority control problems might have on retrieval.

Another decision faced by any library undertaking a conversion project is that of the number of fields to be checked during the project. A decision as to how much checking to do involves a trade--off of accuracy vs. speed. At Winthrop we opted for speed and only checked through the 300 field. There are definite disadvantages to such a decision. We hope, maybe foolishly, that an automated method of updating subject headings will be available before we implement an online catalog. In our case, some inaccurate data got into our database, and some data has been lost.

The most significant item that we did not update is the date element in the fixed field. CLSI uses this field, rather than the date in the imprint, to index entries by date. Errors in the date element occurred frequently before OCLC required users of the "new" command to update that date.

We are not sure if we would check the entire record if we were to do our retrospective conversion project again. One study we did indicated that we picked up as much additional information on our cataloging records as we lost. We do know that we would not yet be finished with the project if we had not stopped with the 300 field. As CLSI has begun the development of an online authority control module which will allow global changes to the bibliographic data file, perhaps our trade off for speed in retrospective conversion will be remedied.

"Bound Withs": Monographic Series

Some other cataloging practices can cause problems. Because two books bound in one cover, the so--called "bound withs" have two bibliographic records, the circulation system will be able to retrieve both titles but only one title will show copy information, as a copy (or item) number can be attached to only one record.

If monographic series titles are not cataloged separately, the only information in the system is for the series. The system will still checkout the books, but the notices sent to patrons will be somewhat incomprehensible to them, as patrons are likely to identify the book by its unique title, not the series title.

Call Numbers

If a library has deviated from standard Library of Congress practices, it may be sorry when it sees its tapes. We do not format our LC call numbers on our cards as they appear on a MARC record. First, we put a period before every Cutter number, not just the first. The OCLC print program will supply the extra periods. The call numbers on the tape do not have them.

This would not be a major problem, if we did not make one other change. We also like to have a space between the letters "I" and "O" and the numbers following them. To obtain this result, we transfer the LC call number to the 099 field. When these call numbers are transferred to CLSI, they *have* the extra period, creating exceptions which used to complicate searching the database by call number. The search enhancement which ignores internal punctuation has eliminated this problem.

For the sake of consistency, this problem can be solved by making sure an 050 or 090 call number exists for every LC number in an 099 field. The program that processes the tapes then selects the 099 field in an LC holding library only when no 090 or 050 exists.

In our juvenile book collection, we suppress call numbers with an "x" in the 090 field. The SOLINET processing program did not recognize this practice and transferred the x's to our CLSI call number field. Those will have to be deleted manually.

One practice to be avoided at all costs is that of not making "minor" changes on the OCLC terminal but rather just typing them on the catalog cards. A significant number of errors we have found were cases where a call number had been corrected when we first started using OCLC and were not aware of all the implications of the archival tape.

"Lost" Records

The last, and potentially most interesting, problem is the "NOT ON FILES." These are records which we have recorded as updated but which did not make it to our SOLINET reformatted tapes. We are willing to concede that our records may be in error when OCLC does not show us as a holding library on a record. But we do not know how to explain the missing records when we are on the record, especially if our shelflist card is an OCLC card!

We do not know if the records got deleted during the many tape copying procedures. We have gathered some examples which SOLINET is using to try to track down the cause. This is more intriguing than alarming as such missing records are a fraction of a percent of the total file.

MARC Tape Input Facility

Finally, an enhancement to the CLSI software, released after our tape load, should make loading MARC tapes much easier. The MARC Tape Input Facility will allow direct loading of OCLC-MARC tapes without prior reformatting. The following exposition is based on the documentation provided by CLSI, not on personal experience with the facility.

The program seems to have provided for all the variables possible in a MARC record. However, the CLSI system is still limited to thirty fields of 512 characters. Print constants are available through a library-specified "literal value" table. Using this, the library can determine what a certain indicator will cause to precede a certain note. Up to 99 literal values, i.e. print constants, may be entered. "Translation tables" may also be defined, which will cause the translation of data in a MARC record to another form before transferring to CLSI. The most obvious example is the OCLC holding library code to the CLSI agency code.

A table may also be defined which tells which MARC fields transfer to which CLSI fields. The transfer can be made conditional, depending upon the material class, indicators, relative position in the record, etc. Several MARC fields can be combined into one CLSI field with library-defined dividing punctuation. Particular subfields may be pulled out or concatenated.

Both old and new style OCLC number prefixes can be handled, and they can be converted to a uniform style if desired. ISN's and LC card numbers can be manipulated. Default values can be specified if data, such as price, is missing from the MARC record.

It is also possible to store full MARC records in addition to the reformatted records. Manipulation of the full record, other than deletion, is not possible at this time.

Unfortunately, the Tape Facility is an extra cost option. The price at this writing was about $15,000, which means Winthrop's 177,717 records would have cost about 8.5 cents each plus about 0.5 cents each for the MARC archival tape records, or about two cents per record more than SOLINET charged. However, for the extra cost a library would have the continuing ability to load MARC tapes. If the file to be converted is 215,000 titles or more, there would be no extra cost. The smaller the file, the greater the extra cost.

OCLC and DataPhase:
Public Library of Charlotte and Mecklenburg County

Carol B. Myers
Head, Technical Services
Public Library of Charlotte and Mecklenburg County

A review of the first four years of an OCLC member's implementation of the DataPhase Automated Library Information System detailing some illustrations of what can go wrong in combining a large bibliographic utility with a turnkey circulation system. The problems discussed deal primarily with technical difficulties of hardware and software in linking the two systems.

The combination of an OCLC member purchasing and utilizing the DataPhase automated circulation system is now a common one. In 1979, however, when the Public Library of Charlotte and Mecklenburg County installed the DataPhase equipment and software, we were one of the first public libraries to do so. Although hardly pioneers, we did encounter some of those difficulties and glitches that pester any new undertaking. Some of these problems were the company's, some were our own, and some arose in the OCLC–DataPhase interface.

Now, five years later, the particular problems themselves often are not very important. However, a review of them gives some perspective on the types of things that can go wrong in combining a large utility with a turnkey circulation system. The problems are interesting as illustrations, but the emphasis should be on the viability of the OCLC and DataPhase combination.

Furthermore, the DataPhase circulation system works, and works well as a circulation system for us in Charlotte, and quite well as a bibliographic system. The Automated Library Information System (ALIS) gives us immediate access to local bibliographic and shelflist information that it would take three of four cumbersome paper files to replicate. We would never willingly go back to a manual cataloging and inventory system.

Background

A brief description of the beginning of the OCLC-DataPhase combination in Charlotte is necessary. The Public Library in Charlotte joined OCLC in 1978 and began using the system in February of 1979. In that same year, our ALIS hardware was delivered and we began our retrospective conversion procedures with a temporary CETA staff. Since then we have converted 210,000 titles out of an estimated 350,000 titles representing 500,000 volumes. All sixteen of our locations are now online and we are finishing the conversion of our stacks and reference collections. All current cataloging is handled through OCLC and sent to ALIS across dedicated telephone lines. We still use the first software package developed by DataPhase called ALIS I.

We had not planned originally to do our retrospective conversion on OCLC, as we do now, but rather with a large commercial vendor. In an arrangement between DataPhase and this vendor, one by-product was to be our ability to hit against the vendor's database. When the two companies could not reach terms (and while we had waited for them), we agreed to DataPhase's recommendation that we begin our conversion project by loading a database that was a hybrid of a public library and a commercial vendor's bibliographic records on one tape into our computer equipment in Charlotte.

The loading of this database was one of our biggest mistakes. The loading itself took several weeks (as did the unloading when we decided that this method would not work) and it it took up precious storage space in our equipment.

The bibliographic records were of an uneven quality due to their various sources. For example, some had been created before the MARC format and OCLC standards were finalized and some were of unknown parentage. Furthermore the titles in the database were not very similar to ours in fact, although they were in theory. We achieved a very poor hit rate against this hybrid database. We soon decided that there had to be a better way.

If you ever have to contend with a non-OCLC database, or one from another library or vendor, explore carefully the quality of the bibliographic records, the fullness of the records, and the compatibility of the titles involved with your collections. If these aspects pass muster, then consider the impact on the storage capabilities of your equipment. Will there be room to build your own files? Finally, consider the possible impact on response time.

In April of 1980, we began our retrospective conversion on OCLC with five additional terminals. As mentioned earlier, we are progressing nicely with it. There was a time before the direct OCLC-ALIS link was possible that we used OCLC archive tapes to transfer bibliographic records to ALIS. In 1979, we ordered from SOLINET a tape covering six months of that year which had 27,000 records on it. After it was loaded, we purchased weekly tapes from OCLC for about seven months until the direct link between the two systems was functioning.

Linking OCLC and DataPhase

Against that background, the kinds of problems we encountered can be seen as examples of similar difficulties to expect, and per-- haps avoid, in such a situation. The problems group themselves into four categories. First, technical problems, that is hardware and software difficulties in combining OCLC and DataPhase. Second, internal DataPhase decisions and programming that caused problems. Third, problems directly related to the records we retained from the hybrid database, and fourth, problems associ- ated with the direct link between the OCLC terminals and the ALIS CPU.

The first problem has to do with the internal codes used in computers for letters and characters called by their acronyms ASCII and EBCDIC. Without explaining the codes themselves, suffice it to say that OCLC and DataPhase use different ones at least part of the time. This variance made it necessary in 1979 for DataPhase to "preprocess" our OCLC–SOLINET tape before we could load it into our computer. Now, local programming eliminates this step. However, at the time, the preprocessing caused us some headaches. Several hundred bibliographic records were lost. They never appeared in ALIS although our holding code remained in OCLC to show we had used the record.
All 092 and 099 Dewey classification numbers were put into an 090 tag. If we ever produce a COM catalog or use a tape from ALIS, we will have to sort out the local Dewey from local LC classification numbers.
Lastly, the preprocessing caused a minor, albeit nagging, pro- blem by changing all square brackets into the letters "t" and "l". Other special characters from the ALA character set also underwent changes.

Another technical difficulty concerns the density of the in- formation of the OCLC tapes we loaded. This density is expressed as "characters per inch" or CPI. OCLC produces tapes at 1600 CPI and our DataPhase equipment loads tapes at 800 CPI. One can ask OCLC to produce a less dense tape at 800 CPI but there is a charge per tape to do so. If a dual density tape drive had been part of our hardware configuration, this problem would not have come up.

Some weekly tapes we received from OCLC were blank by the time we shipped them on to DataPhase for preprocessing. We did not discover that problem when we received them since we were unable to load them directly. Unfortunately, by the time we sent them to DataPhase for preprocessing and they were returned, our warranty had run out.

Another technical problem concerns piece-specific or item information in the 049 field. In the ALIS I software, the subfield codes are defined differently by DataPhase than by OCLC. Therefore, if one creates an 049 for specific holdings by OCLC standards and subfields, it will not work in ALIS and *vice versa*.

A minor technical difficulty involves the formatting of the screen display in OCLC and ALIS. The same record will not appear in exactly the same way on the two systems. For example, the DataPhase screen can display words split between two lines or begin lines with punctuation marks instead of ending the preceeding line with them.

A more important technical problem that has not been resolved involves the lag between an OCLC change in format and the rewriting of DataPhase software to accomplish that change. For instance, the fixed field for TEXT has been changed to ACCOMPANYING MATERIAL in the scores format. DataPhase ALIS I software has not made that change and we cannot load or send any bibliographic records for musical scores from OCLC to ALIS without manually changing the new words to the old word on the screen and correcting the spacing. Without this manual change, the records are kicked into the error file or stop the batch process.

There may be similar problems in other less used formats as well. DataPhase was reluctant to spend the time to change ALIS I software when ALIS II would soon be available for ALIS I sites to load.

Three general technical problems finish this first list. They are (1) it takes a long time to load a tape and response time is often affected while it is loading, (2) storing and "refreshing" tapes have special requirements; and (3) if a computer configuration has only one tape drive, the log tape cannot run while an OCLC tape is loading.

DataPhase Programming and Decisions

ALIS I software does not accept diacritical marks other than the standard English language ones. If bibliographic records have other such marks, they are all changed "b" 's or "h" 's thereby causing some titles or main entries to be unsearchable. DataPhase has no plans to implement a full ALA character set, citing cost considerations. If tapes are loaded, the diacritical marks are deleted automatically by DataPhase software. However, with the direct link, they are not deleted but appear as other characters. Therefore, we delete all foreign diacritical marks before sending to ALIS to avoid problems.

We found early on that bibliographic records with no Library of Congress card number were causing us problems. The DataPhase system, in an effort to avoid duplicate records matches an incoming OCLC record against any record already in the system with the same vendor number and LC card number. If there is no LC card number, the system looks at all the others with no card number (in our case this became 2,000 or so before we caught on). This procedure slows the batch process by hours for each one unless the operator tells the system not to check by card number.

Our first attempt to cope with the problem led us to batch process all records without an LC card number together until we learned the easier way. Obviously, learning to operate a circulation system and recognize its subtleties takes some time.

As is true perhaps in many situations, we have found a wide gap between what we understood the salesman to say and what the programmers and operators say now. DataPhase does have a strong users' group where one may share concerns and lobby for change, as well as learn how others have solved problems. And of course, it is only human nature that, having heard of the feasibility of some enhancement to want it immediately.

The company is now testing and making available a whole new software package called ALIS II. No doubt many of our problem situations will not be encountered in the new software. On the other hand, we may have a whole new set to learn and with which to contend. We are going to let another library be first this time and wait to load ALIS II until some of the initial bugs have been worked out.

Using Another Database

The bibliographic records in the hybrid database mentioned earlier were of an uneven quality as they were created under varying standards by a number of different libraries and vendors. Some of the records were in a pre–MARC format and others were very brief. As we had decided on a minimum level of cataloging that was fuller than some of these records, we had to edit and upgrade them.

One of our nagging problems is that we cannot get rid of these hybrid records by using the automatic bumping program that works for OCLC records. That is, a later OCLC update of a record will bump the earlier one in ALIS after establishing it describes the same bibliographic item by checking vendor number, LC card number, and so on. The hybrid records have no vendor number. They don't even have a leader. We have to manually switch holdings from the hybrid to the correct OCLC record and then delete the hybrid record manually. This switching is a time consuming process.

Direct Link Between OCLC and ALIS

If a library began today to use the DataPhase system in conjunction with OCLC, it would probably not load OCLC archive tapes to transfer bibliographic information for current cataloging. Instead it would use the direct software and telephone line link from the OCLC screen to ALIS memory. Bibliographic records are sent and stored in ALIS until an overnight batch "translates" the incoming information. Then it can be recorded in memory and found through ALIS's dictionaries. Some of the problems with this procedure have already been mentioned and include the loss of the ability to clean up diacriticals automatically. Others are:

We had to slow down transmission from 1200 baud to 300 baud on our OCLC terminals and printer. At the faster rate the information received in ALIS was garbled.

We occasionally have character loss, not whole fields or necessarily even words, usually just a character here or there. This happens only infrequently and usually when the system is being heavily used.

Searching for bibliographic records in ALIS to add holdings information for an item slows the whole system down. We found the slow response time for circulation transactions unacceptable and to make it better, we have had to upgrade and add to our equipment twice.

Conclusion

In summary, there are four groups of problems we faced. Some are attributable to us at the Public Library of Charlotte and Mecklenburg County; some, to DataPhase; and some, to the interface of the circulation system with OCLC. But, the two can be blended and work very well together.

We now have with ALIS a solid circulation system, the benefits of multiple access points in an online system, better inventory control, and the future capability of global authority work -- all of which is based on a bibliographic record created through OCLC.

The kinds of difficulties we encountered show that there are bugs to be worked out of a new system or the combination of systems, but the benefits we have gained outweigh the problems. DataPhase and OCLC form a workable and productive team.

Processing OCLC Archive Tapes for the FOCUS System:
University of Florida

Nolan F. Pope
Head, Systems and Computer–Based Operations
University of Florida Libraries

Some of the issues addressed in the processing of the OCLC archive tapes for the University of Florida Libraries' online catalog are discussed. Emphasis is primarily on those issues which are common to many libraries' archive tapes and to most automated systems. Changes in the OCLC system, local procedures, and cataloging rules which affect the processing are illustrated.

The Florida Online Computerized User System (FOCUS) is the University of Florida Libraries' automated system for internal and public access to the Libraries' collections. FOCUS is based on the NOTIS system from Northwestern University and is designed to support all of the Libraries' operations: acquisitions, serials control, authority control, circulation, and an online catalog. Some 380,000 OCLC archive tape records from catalog processing and retrospective conversion projects comprise the initial database of the union catalog. Other databases supported by the system are not derived from OCLC records but are based on MARC-formatted records.

The University Libraries first addressed the processing of the archive tapes in 1979 for a COM catalog and for the installation of a CLSI circulation system which was later withdrawn. The former was designed to be a complete catalog, rather than a series of brief entries, but it was not intended to replace the card catalog. The COM catalog existed as a supplement in library locations which are remote from the card catalogs.

The COM catalog processing, since it required full catalog records for all main entries, involved much of the same processing that is required for the FOCUS online system. That processing was specified and contracted with the intent that the resulting machine readable records would be used for the online database as well as for the COM. Therefore, the initial load of the database involved those archive tapes processed for the COM by Auto–

Graphics, Inc. That processing resolved such problems as combining later occurrences of a record, whether updates or deletes, linking locations to call numbers, and standardizing some inconsistencies in the early archive tapes. Subsequent OCLC archive tapes are loaded directly into FOCUS as they are received, and FOCUS load programs handle the "cumulating" of information to an existing title record.

The University Libraries

The University Libraries comprise a large library system, encompassing four processing centers, numerous branches and reading rooms, and several specialized collections. Each of the four processing centers has a separate OCLC profile. Three follow the Library of Congress practices and subject headings for most of their collections; the fourth, the Health Center Library, adheres to National Library of Medicine policies and uses the Medical Subject Heading (MeSH) terms.

The OCLC terminals were installed in 1975 and 1976, except for the Health Center Library, which began using OCLC in 1981. It earlier used the NLM Catline for cataloging copy, but that system did not generate archive tapes of records being used. Until 1979, no use of continual maintenance in the form of cumulating in--coming OCLC archive tape records was developed by the University Libraries.

The Archive Data

Using the OCLC archive data required a cumulation of the records as they appeared on the archive tapes and the processing of the records according to the specific OCLC profile which generated them. Coupled with the need to identify the local uses of fields, a written specification for that processing was prepared. Changes in practices locally, system changes by OCLC over the past eight years, and complications from "dirty data" had to be considered.

One of the first and most difficult areas to address related to the early practice of placing on a single record all copy and location information relating to that title. The main library Catalog Department processes materials for several branches and collections, using several classification schemes. Between the four processing centers, over four hundred OCLC 049 codes represent the various locations, classification schemes and forms of materials. Therefore, if multiple location codes are present in the 049 field, the system must link each to the appropriate call number field. However, if there were multiple 099 fields, a combination of 099 and 090, or 099 and 092, it was impossible to know which related to which location (figure 1).

In processing those records, the end result was that those which could not be resolved by a machine algorithm had to be edited by library staff. Fortunately, the Catalog Department staff had realized the potential problems of this practice, and beginning in late 1976, a separate bibliographic record was created for each location code if different call numbers were used. Therefore, subsequent processing cumulated all occurrences of single OCLC number and location code combinations, rather than simply watching for subsequent occurrences of the OCLC number to replace the earlier record.

Processing the 099 field also revealed a wide variety of practices (figure 2). It contained free text, the K schedules, modified classification schemes, and notations at the beginning of call numbers, such as Ref or R for Reference, f for Folio, or B for biographies. The main library Catalog Department has separate OCLC profiles for Dewey and Library of Congress classification schemes. However, Dewey call numbers were sometimes entered in the 099 of the L.C. profile, and L.C. numbers appeared in the 099 of the Dewey profile. Non--L.C. call numbers may begin with letters for some materials, meaning that a simple test of the first character will not separate the classification schemes. Specialized processing was necessary which considered location code, the initial parsing values of call numbers, and the presence or absence of conversion codes in the 035 or the 910 fields.

Call number processing affects various issues: these include shelflist sorts, formatting for displays, and generating indexes for searching. An "R" preceding a Dewey number was changed to a 049 location code for Reference, and the call number was reformatted without the "R" (figure 3). Library of Congress numbers from the 050 and the 099 fields had to be normalized since the 050 places the letters and numbers of the classification in a single subfield and the 099 places each segment in repeating subfields (figure 4). The catalog user must not be confronted with differentiating between the two. For shelflist sorts, certain segments must be left--justified and others right--justified, regardless of how they are formatted in the 050 versus the 099.

Data Accuracy

The basic accuracy of the data is naturally a major concern. The University Libraries realized that not all corrections had been made online; the taboo practice of only changing the card and

Figure 1

When a single record contains multiple call number fields and 049 location codes, it may not be possible to determine the appropriate call number and location combinations via machine processing. The following example shows four location codes and three call numbers; the 092 and 099 fields are valid call number fields for any of the location codes in this record.

```
092   912.7595 ‡b W878a
099   912.759 ‡a W878a ‡a 1974
099   R ‡a 912.759 ‡a Woo
049   fugy ‡c 1 ‡a fugf ‡c 1 ‡a fuga ‡c 1 ‡a fugr
      [Another] [Copy] [912.7595] [W878a] [Arch &]
      [Fine Arts] ‡c 1
```

Figure 2

The 099 field may have several types of call numbers, including text.

099   B ‡a C763   (This would be a biography.)

099   B ‡a 458 ‡a .E5 ‡a R67 ‡a 1974 (This is a LC call number since the field following the B begins with a number instead of the letter of a cutter.)

099   R516.592 ‡a C562   (This is a Dewey call number for a Reference collection title.)

099   R ‡a 516.67 ‡a .H34   (This is a LC call number in the R schedule. The R stands alone as a separate subfield.)

099   HN863.4 ‡a F345n   (This is a Dewey number with a letter prefix showing the country of publication for 86X items in the Latin American collection.)

099   HN ‡a 863.4 ‡a .F345n   (This is a LC call number. The HN stands as a separate subfield in the 099.)

099   T-108 ‡a Tape   (This number and text indicates a cassette tape.)

099   f ‡a 99.23 ‡a N935a   (In the FUA profile, the f indicates a folio. In the FUG profile, the f indicates the title is in the Florida History collection.)

Figure 3

Machine manipulation of reference call numbers to transfer the collection indication to the location code instead of being a part of the call number.

049   fugg
099   R823.2 ‡a B634a

changed to:

049   fugr
099   823.2 ‡b B634a

Figure 4

Format variations for LC call numbers in the 050 field versus the 099.

050   HQ34.6 ‡b .T38
099   HQ ‡a 34.6 ‡a .T38

Figure 5

Filing indicators.

245 _ 4 The Wind and the Stars

The second indicator value of 4 means that the title is indexed and searchable under the word "Wind", not "The".

sending it off to the catalog was a reality. However, in most cases where it was realized that the error involved a searchable field of the record, error reports were completed and filed. These have been used in editing the online database.

The issue of copy and volume information in the record was also addressed if available. However, local practices did not include keeping complete copy information in the machine readable records; subsequent copies added to the same locations were simply noted on the shelflist card.

Volume information was input through the system when the record was created, but added volumes to that title which did not require additional cards were simply noted on the shelflist and in the catalog. As a result, the archive tapes do not necessarily reflect shelflist data of holdings for an individual title. This policy was adopted primarily because the archive tapes represented only a portion of the collection, and adding the copy and volume data through OCLC was too expensive in terms of transaction costs and the requisite man-hours.

Another problem which plagues online systems is the filing indicator (figure 5). Initially, it was not available through the OCLC system, so all early records lack it. It is an easy thing to overlook, and it is occasionally omitted in current records. Also, it is not available for some added entry fields.

After analyzing the archive records, it was evident that adding filing indicators via terminal keyboarding was unacceptable due to the number of changes needed. Programs were developed to set the filing indicators for specified fields. Due to problems of letter combinations representing an article in one language and a non-article in another, the language code for the record identified the possible articles which should be detected.

Problems Arising from Reclassification

Reclassification projects created some interesting tape processing problems. Following the change from Dewey to the L.C. classification scheme in 1977, it was decided to reclassify the Reference Collection in the main library. Some of the collection's titles were on the 1975 to 1977 Dewey profile tapes; others were not. The change to the L.C. classification meant adding a new set of location codes to the OCLC profile so that each collection now has the earlier Dewey code and the new L.C. code.

Reclassification meant that the titles entered under the new L.C. profile code had to be linked to the earlier occurrence under the Dewey profile code. If the link was not made, the title then appeared as having two copies; both in Reference, but one with a

Dewey number (which no longer existed), and one with a L.C. number. However, if the reclassification staff did not use the same OCLC record as was used when cataloged under the Dewey scheme, the OCLC number match for combining the records failed.

In processing the archive tapes, special consideration should be given to any conversion projects which were instrumental in adding large numbers of titles to the database. The most important point to determine is whether or not the quality control was consistent with the procedures of initial cataloging, and if not, where the differences are. Conversion projects frequently produce no printed products such as catalog cards. This eliminates the review process to detect errors in spelling or tagging of fields.

The University of Florida Libraries had a major project in 1975 for converting all frequently circulating items from the main library. Although headed by a cataloger, the project was not under the Catalog Department supervision or near their tools, and some quality controls were not imposed. One valuable feature in processing the records was having a conversion code placed in the 035 field for all converted records. That helped signal the need for special processing in selecting and formatting call numbers which later emerged as a problem.

As a result of these experiences, all future conversion projects will be closely controlled by the Libraries' Catalog Departments. "Quick and dirty" approaches haunt the database with unexplainable inaccuracies. In the long term, it takes less time and money to include quality controls initially.

As we cumulated the archive tapes we had to address some collection mergers which had been effected after the 1975 implementation of OCLC. The undergraduate collection was integrated into the research collection after designated blocks of call numbers were transferred to the Music Library and the Architecture and Fine Arts Library. The machine processing had to change the 049 location codes to those of the new holding libraries after sorting by call number.

The use of location-specific bibliographic data for titles is also being addressed in the loading of the FOCUS database. One of the most obvious relates to the subject headings used for the Map Library's collection. The reversed geographic heading is a common practice among map libraries. Unfortunately it abrogates all authority control of L.C. subject headings if merged into the Libraries' Union Catalog.

To resolve this problem, the Map Library record is entered in OCLC with the appropriate 049 code and the term "map" in the 035 field. The same OCLC record is then used again, this time also with the Map Library code, but with standard L.C.

subject headings. In FOCUS, a single record is used, retaining the two sets of subject headings but changing the second indicator value of the Map Library subject fields (figure 6). FOCUS allows for separate subject indexes, according to the Libraries' definition of the second indicator. For example, the common L.C.--controlled index for the names and series entries of records can have separate subject indexes for L.C. Subject Headings, MeSH terms, and the geographic headings for the maps.

Figure 6

Merging unique subject headings from various records.

650_0 ǂa Geology ǂz Wyoming ǂz Natrona Co. ǂx Maps
651_4 ǂa Natrona Co., Wyo. ǂx Geology ǂx Maps

Both subject heading fields will be merged onto a single bibliographic record. Based on the Map Library 049 code and a conversion phrase in the 035 field, the Map Library records' subject heading field indicators will be changed to a value of 4. Based on that indicator, those subject headings will be part of a separate subject index.
The title and author indexes, however, are shared for the two collections.

The same technique will identify MeSH terms and enter them in that index. The same record could have LC Subject Heading index entries if any of the 6XX fields have a second indicator value of 0.

Changes: MARC, OCLC, Catalog Rules

Most changes to the MARC formats have been in the form of new tags or subfields, at least within the 1975 to 1983 time frame. There is no significant problem with loading new field tags such as 007, or new MARC formats such as authority or manuscripts formats, into FOCUS. The system accepts them as part of variable length records with variable occurrences of fields. New tags are added to the system tables, allowing the software to operate according to that data. For example, it can then retrieve that field of information, can limit displays as a function of the field values, and can format that data separately. Basically, FOCUS follows the USMARC formats and the ALA Character Set.

Considering the importance of the 049 field to the processing of the archive records, past OCLC system changes regarding this field are crucial. Initially, if the 049 field was displayed on the OCLC terminal screen as a default value of the profile, the PRO-DUCE/SEND or UPDATE/SEND function did not transfer the 049 value to the archive tape with the other fields of data.

Initial processing of these records showed that they had no 049 present in them, and therefore could not proceed through the call number selection routines of the programs to show holdings information. The default value for the given profile had to be inserted into the 049 prior to that step in the programs. Also during the initial stages of OCLC, the 049 codes were three letters instead of the four--letter ones used now. The processing had to insert a letter between the second and third characters.

Another problem facing all libraries that began using OCLC prior to January 1981 is the AACR-1 versus AACR-2 issue. The University of Florida Libraries did not choose to upgrade any pre-1981 archive tape records via OCLC, even though changes made to the card catalogs identified OCLC-produced records with the now incorrect form or choice of heading. Records of these were made in the AACR-2 authority file, and the FOCUS software capability for making global changes will facilitate this process. The authority file records can also indicate existing index records which will match with invalid cross references of the AACR-2 authority records. Batch listings of these conflicts will help resolve these inconsistencies.

System Specific Problems and Issues

Basically, it must be realized that the 049 codes and the use of bracketed information in the 049 field are OCLC conventions for showing location above or below the catalog card's call number. The bracketed information is translated into a FOCUS record location or sub-location. However, there are problems in that the bracketed information may have spelling or formatting errors, resulting in a non-match against the translation table of possibilities. Since the bracketed information is free text, there are occasionally problems with abbreviating it into the collection name fields.

In some combinations, the bracketed information is unnecessary in a union database. For example, when cataloging a copy for the Education Library, bracketed information may state that another copy is held in the Main Library. This is obviously valuable to the users of the Education Library's card catalog. However, in a single integrated database of all the Libraries' holdings, that note is redundant since the Main and Education locations will be linked to the same bibliographic record. Processing ignored certain bracketed phrases, but problems were still encountered with non-standard formatting, misspelling, and non-standard abbreviations.

The OCLC record leader also has some differences from the USMARC counterpart. For example, OCLC recognizes a record type of "h" for items originally published as microforms. This is not recognized by USMARC, and thus was not initially in the FOCUS table as a valid record type.

The concept of UPDATE/SEND and PRODUCE/SEND are OCLC conventions represented in the bytes of the record leader. Since UPDATE/SEND is often the distinguishing factor of conversion project records, processing may be varied for those records. If nothing else, those records may need closer scrutiny since they produced no printed products for quality control review.

The OCLC record number is the primary constant within that system for its database operations. However, in the FOCUS system, the FOCUS record number, which is system generated, performs that function. This is typical of all systems, but it requires changing the role of the OCLC number when loading it into the local system. In FOCUS, the OCLC number resides in the 035 field, with a prefix of the OCLC's NUC code. This practice is described in the USMARC documentation for local numbers.[1]

Documentation for Local Practices

When the University of Florida Libraries began using OCLC, no detailed or comprehensive record of system or procedural changes was maintained. Some of the issues which later caused problems with processing the tapes were never perceived as potential problems; others simply were not thoroughly documented. Much of this was undoubtedly due to not knowing exactly how the archive tapes would be used in the future and also not being familiar with database processing issues.

The Catalog Department staff had earlier expressed concern about the archive tapes, feeling somewhat in limbo as to how they would be used and whether or not the existing procedures were creating reliable data. These concerns led to procedural changes, such as no longer placing all copy/location information on a single bibliographic record if the different location codes were linked to different call numbers, different notes, or various other copy--specific pieces of information.

To process the OCLC archive tapes, it was necessary to remedy the gap in procedural documentation. Preparation of specifications for processing the OCLC archive tapes relied on the memories of the Catalog Department staff. Fortunately, the catalogers responsible for the installation, profiling, and implementation of OCLC into each of the Catalog Departments are still at the University. Using that source of information, the specifications were written by the Department of Systems and Computer-Based Operations.

Summary

The University of Florida Libraries have successfully used the OCLC archive tapes to generate a machine-readable database for the FOCUS system. This required the writing of specifications to detail the Libraries' use of OCLC, all procedures, variations for special projects, and the characteristics of individual collections. This analysis also assisted in determining if current procedures needed to be altered to avoid continual problems with processing future tapes.

---

[1] U.S. Library of Congress. Automated Systems Office. *MARC Formats for Bibliographic Data.* Washington, D.C.: Library of Congress, 1980-.

OCLC Tapes and the Development of a Local System: University of Alabama in Birmingham

Jerry W. Stephens
Assistant Director for Administrative Services
The University of Alabama in Birmingham

The decision to use OCLC tapes in a locally developed system will affect the design of that system. The methods employed to implement the system at the University of Alabama in Birmingham, such as staff involvement and retrospective conversion are discussed.

The use of OCLC tape records is important to the design and functioning of a local system. This application has many implications for both vendor--supplied and user--developed systems. The use of the records provided by the shared cataloging system is one, if not the major source of data for building a local database. There are many advantages and disadvantages to the use of the OCLC tape records. This is not to say that the same problems would not occur in the use of records supplied from another vendor, or that the solutions applicable to the OCLC tapes would not apply to tapes of other vendors.

In considering the use of magnetic tape records from any source, several points are quite important. First, the structure of the record is important, as it allows for machine use of the record in a consistent and prescribed method. This consideration is important in reducing the number and kind of problems one might encounter when transforming the tape record to an online database record.

The source and structure of the data used in constructing the online database is very important in designing and implementing a local system. Consideration of this source data should occur in the planning stages of the system design and not as an afterthought, when changes might be cumbersome or even impossible. Early consideration and planning can greatly reduce the problems encountered in the conversion of records into a machine readable format, as well as in the creation of the local database from a machine readable source.

The staff at The University of Alabama in Birmingham, Sterne

Library (U.A.B.) learned early in the use of OCLC as a cataloging source that the method and form of the records must be maintained in a very precise manner. Because of this, the changes in the OCLC profile, as well as the implementation of local practices, have been carefully documented. Certain information, local in nature and thought to be important initially, was discarded as refinements in the online system progressed. This includes data such as price and date cataloged.

Because of the importance placed on this structured environment by the local system, changes to the OCLC profile for the institutional records are considered very carefully. The use of the shared cataloging system is more than simply identifying what items are in the library's collection. The magnetic record must provide an accurate representation of the item to insure the integrity of the online databases. These concerns are important because of the ability of the online local system to index the record properly. This is critical because records are indexed at the point of insertion, and these indexes are used in the retrieval search strategies.

Use of the OCLC tapes at U.A.B. has been very satisfactory. The computer center staff was extremely helpful in the design and implementation of the conversion project tapes, and in the use of the weekly update tapes, both of which were used to create the circulation database. The weekly update tapes assist in maintaining the information necessary for an online, interactive, short entry catalog.

The local database was constructed using the OCLC system. Records of holdings were identified in the OCLC system and were captured on the archival tapes. These records were then used to construct the online database. Since the conversion was a title record and not a conversion of holdings information, the title record for each set or multicopy situation was captured without holdings information. As the physical volumes were tagged with the circulation control number, the local system record was updated to show all holdings information. This updating was done by appending multiple circulation control records to the OCLC title record, which reduced the amount of duplicate information stored in the online databases.

In an effort to overcome changes in the OCLC tape format since 1975, SOLINET provided U.A.B. with a single run of approximately 135,000 title records, on magnetic tape, in shelflist order. This arrangement was requested to minimize the problems involved in labeling the collection as it was loaded in the local database. Copy specific information was not converted but was later added using the local online edit routine.

The labeling of the collection was done by allowing the machine to match a title with a circulation control number. The computer generated the control label for the book and an edit list to help the staff properly identify the book cited. Physical units other than part one, volume one, copy one of the title were added online by the library staff.

Simultaneous to the conversion of the historical machine readable data into the online database, items being cataloged using the shared cataloging system were being edited to include the circulation system control number in the 049 field. This allowed the maintenance of the local database to move into its final form as rapidly as possible. This change occurred so that it became effective on a particular day, thus allowing the computer staff to identify the particular tape that changed format. The local system handled the format change without problems because the library and computer center staffs understood the implications of such changes and planned for them.

The approach taken at U.A.B. is probably not unique. Likewise, it is probably not transportable to another site in its entirety without some modification. Different computer centers and libraries have uniquenesses which must be considered in an effort of this type. Good lines of communication must exist between the computer center staff servicing the library system and the library staff. Poor communication can destroy the project from the outset.

Many automated systems fail not because they are bad applications, but because the manual interface to the automated system is poor. Successful interaction with the automated system is critical in the development of quality service, and staff and user acceptance. The manual procedures must present a logical progression from manual procedures to automated interaction.

Personnel are an important part of any system, automated or not. The success of an automated system is highly dependent on the personnel involved. An important aspect in that involvement is the satisfaction the staff members are able to derive from the work they perform. U.A.B's technical processing staff members are now able to see a product which is representative of their work. It is the record in the local online database. It is an institutional record and not the master OCLC record.

The importance and use of this record versus the OCLC record helps to motivate the staff to perform at a higher level of accuracy. This local online database also allows the technical services staff to see the implication of poor performance by themselves and other staff members.

The library staff must be able to formulate their wishes and needs in a manner that is understandable and practical to the systems analyst. The analyst has the responsibility to communicate logical reasons for alternative approaches to the library's requests. Both parties must consider each other's needs and constraints, and must reach an acceptable compromise when necessary.

The use of a local online system is probably within the planning horizons of every library. The success or failure of the system and its services rests not just with the technicians who design and implement the applications programs, but with the librarians and other users, as well.

COM Catalog Maintenance Considerations:
Georgia State University

Christina Landram
Head, Catalog Department
Georgia State University

Problems of maintenance in a COM catalog when cataloging is done through a bibliographic utility are discussed. Problems regarding filing indicators, series entries, computer programs of the COM vendor vs. those of the bibliographic utility, and maintenance of a machine readable catalog are explored.

This is a discussion of the problems discovered in the COM catalog at Georgia State University resulting from the use of OCLC. Some of the problems we encountered were due to things beyond our control, but some were due to our ignorance or lack of foresight.
On receipt of the COM catalog at Georgia State we established a list of thirteen projects which needed to be accomplished to clean up the machine readable records in our database and therefore the COM catalog.
The procedure used in all changes was to print off the record from the OCLC terminal, make the necessary changes on the printout, and then re--edit the OCLC record from the printout. The printout was then filed.

System and Cataloging Changes

Those of you who have cataloged online using OCLC for many years may remember that in the early days filing indicators were not used in the 245 field. The Library of Congress had always used this filing indicator but OCLC member contributed copy did not. Consequently we were aware that many titles which began with an article were going to file under that article. When the COM arrived, we went through it looking for access points under English articles and articles in major European languages. These were corrected.
One major factor which many people do not recognize is that much of the data on catalog cards from OCLC is due to the print program for cards. A COM vendor may or may not have programs which utilize information as does OCLC. One problem

we encountered related to input stamps in the 049 tag. We have several serials in which the latest issue only is in the Reference collection and the phrase "Reference has only the latest issue" was used as an input stamp. The COM vendor could not print this information and we had to re-do 600 serial titles to move that phrase from the 049 tag to a 590, local note tag.

We have many law books in our collection and in order to shelve books regarding law in countries for which the Library of Congress has not yet developed a classification schedule together with those for which they have developed classifications, we used the same feature that other libraries use of assigning only the class letters for the country and then using a cutter number based on the author followed by a work letter from the first word of the title.

In the early days OCLC allowed us to input this in an 090 call number using K0 (zero) to make it behave like an LC call number. OCLC suppressed the *0* in its card print program. Later, we input this type of call number in the 099 tag. Since the COM vendor did not have a program to suppress the *0*, any of the law numbers which included that character printed it. All these were identified and changed.

Another problem were those series under pre-AACR 2 rules in which the author in the main entry was also the author of the series. That series was entered as "His . . . " or "Her . . . " or "Its . . . " Once more, OCLC's print program accommodated this, but the COM vendor did not, so that several series were filed not under the author's name but under *His, Her,* and *Its*. These have been corrected.

We had also used an input stamp to indicate that we had copies in the stacks and in the reference collection. Retrieving these would have meant going through the entire shelflist card by card. It was decided to handle them as they surfaced.

Problems with Subject Headings

Another problem involved certain famous people used as subject headings. At one time, when certain persons were used as subject headings by the Library of Congress, the birth and death dates of that person were omitted. After all, George Washington, Abraham Lincoln and William Shakespeare were known to all. However, LC subsequently changed this policy and began to add these dates. In our card catalog, we ignored the fact that some entries had dates and other did not and interfiled the entries. The computer will not do that since it files character by character. There were approximately 30 such persons. These access points were checked and corrected if necessary.

Problems We Created

There were also problems we created. Our most serious one was that we did not update our machine readable record. If errors surfaced, we changed the information only on the catalog cards. As the Library of Congress issued the law classifications we had reclassified books into the K,KD and KE classes. We had changed the call number on the books and the catalog cards but not in the machine readable record.

As a result, when our COM arrived we had entries listed with incorrect call numbers. We were able to retrieve these through our shelflist so that those call numbers could be corrected.

We had transferred books into and out of the reference collection and had not changed the machine record. We needed a classed list in order to check it against the reference shelflist to retrieve these items. We used the 2nd edition of the classed catalog to do so. These records have finally been corrected.

Series entries posed several problems. We had not been consistent in using an abbreviation prior to a number in the series entry. If the publisher called one "number" and the next one "volume," we used those terms. They were ignored in the card catalog and the series entries were filed by number only.

The computer, however, does not ignore these terms and if the terms are not consistent, separate lists will be printed. Not only had we used *no.* and *vol.* but also *v.* Since the computer considers a space as a character, spacing was also a problem. We were able to get a list of our series entries from SOLINET and we are in the process of creating a COM series authority file, correcting series entries as this is built. We are about 2/3 complete with this project.

AACR 2 has compounded the problem since it provided for entry under title in more instances as well as the use of uniform titles. Another list of series was generated by our COM vendor in 1983. Unfortunately authority control will not convert series entries.

The completion of the abbreviation problem and the converting of older entries under corporate body to a uniform title is a massive project. No date has been set for its completion. Of 643 usable answers in a survey of patrons by Catalog Department staff in the summer of 1983, 4.5% indicated that they often searched under series entries; and 18% indicated that they sometimes did, while 77.5% seldom or never used them. On the basis of this lack of use, we have not designated converting series as a top priority.

One small maintenance problem concerns garbage which prints at the beginning or end of the file. Compared to our other problems, there was very little of this to clean up.

Names, Subject Headings Lists

Our vendor furnished us with several lists with our first COM. One of these was a Names List, which consisted of over 9000 computer printed sheets listing names used as access points, together with the OCLC number in which that access point appeared. Support staff read these sheets looking for obvious incorrect entries. We located 1577 access points to be corrected. While no record was kept of the number of records this represented, I would estimate that it involved 2300–2500 records.

The vendor also supplied a list of certain subject headings which surfaced due to subject authority control. One of these is an exceptions list and gives subject headings which are not found in the LC subject heading list. These were due to our errors, e.g. ADVERTISINGS – LAWS, and had to be corrected.

Another list of headings were those in which LC had split one heading into two, e.g. NURSES AND NURSING into the separate headings NURSES and NURSING. The computer did not know which titles belonged under which heading. As a result we must change them manually.

There are changes primarily involving AACR 2 still to be made. The vendor applied name authority control to our catalog in June 1983. This generated 3949 pages of computer printout listing 70,948 unique terms not matching LC. This exceptions list was checked against our authority file, which consists of names not in the LC authority file at the time of cataloging. The terms to be corrected were marked and we are about half way completed with this second mammoth correction of records.

On–Going File Maintenance

There is a certain amount of on–going maintenance which we perform. We do not input copy specific information, but we do input summary serials holdings including using that option which is sometimes used in serial card catalogs for those serials on standing order. We use *v. . . . – To date.* However, if we fill in back volumes we go back and change the record. If a title ceases we add that information to a serial record. And of course, when a serial title changes we input a new record and go back and change the old record by adding the appropriate note and closing out the entry.

We are currently cataloging from an edit list since our periodical shelflist is in the public area. That is a copy of our serials records which includes fixed field information and tags just as the record looks on the OCLC screen. SOLINET produced the first list for us, but currently it is being produced by our own computer center from the master file which comes with each catalog.

There are also transfers from the reference collection to be completed. Our Reference Department has been engaged in a massive weeding project, and so we are holding many titles to be transferred.

We do have an error report form which is used by the public service staff whenever an error is located. This has been of great help to us in identifying errors to be corrected.

Cards were pulled from the card catalog for the titles in the COM catalog and the space in the cabinet drawers was eliminated.

Summary

Our greatest need at this time is some method for us to change records so that the entire record does not have to be re--edited through OCLC. At times, all that may be needed is to change one character. However, any method to do this must also provide for a copy of that corrected record to be sent to the COM vendor to replace the incorrect record in our COM. Maintaining records through OCLC is time consuming, and hopefully a faster method can be found.

One of our goals in moving to a COM catalog was the opportunity to clean up our machine readable file. We believe that we have moved a long way toward achieving that goal. Continued maintenance of that file is requisite to sustaining its long worked for quality.

Database Maintenance:
University of Alabama in Birmingham

Jerry W. Stephens
Assistant Director for Administrative Services
The University of Alabama in Birmingham

Database management which has been a primary concern throughout the development and implementation of the local library system is described. The primary areas of concern are security, back-up, storage of historical records, batch updating, and online updating of the database. The integrity and consistent use of data input is important.

The automated library system at the Sterne Library, University of Alabama in Birmingham is an interactive, online acquisitions and circulation system. It has been operational since the Spring of 1980 and has proven to be very satisfactory in meeting the needs of the library user community. The system is a cooperative effort of the University's Computer Center staff and the library staff, and allows online data entry, record editing and database management.

The automated system is supported by an IBM 4341-II. This is the University's main administrative computer which supports university functions such as purchasing, payroll, personnel, accounts payable, a student information system, and various research projects. The computer supports communication management systems such as TSO, CICS and IMS. The library system is designed and functions under the IMS/DC communications management system in the MVS/SP operating system. All applications programs, both online and batch, are in COBOL. These programs were written by the computer center staff based on conceptual and detailed design specifications developed by a task force of library and computer center staff.

The decision to use the University's computer center was made by the University Administration. Alternatives such as mini's or turnkey vendors were explored but later discarded for various reasons. The current situation has proven to be very advantageous to the library because of the interaction with other units using the same machine.

The library system is an interactive information system designed to perform specific functions including acquisitions and circulation. The use of the system and the maintenance of the databases are shared functions. The responsibility for data integrity and security is vested with the computer center staff; data entry and data specification are vested with the technical services personnel in the library.

The development of an in–house system is a major undertaking. It is a task that cannot be dealt with only in passing. The experience at the University of Alabama in Birmingham with a project of this nature was a challenge for the computer center and library staffs. From the beginning of the design phase, database management was a primary concern in the design of the system. The maintenance considerations included both the addition of new records and the editing and deletion of current records, thereby keeping the databases a true representation of the collection. Probably the question that is asked most often about such a system is, "How do you maintain a system of this size and complexity?" In answering this question the response can be segmented into several areas.

Maintaining Dynamic Systems

The first area is that of data integrity and security. This maintenance is performed by the computer center personnel. The functions included in this area are data backup, both on and off site storage and historical record storage.

The second area concerning maintenance is the addition of new records into the online database. This procedure was designed in the initial stages of development. By its structure, it provides for changes in the OCLC profile or MARC format. These changes can be dealt with easily as they occur. Use of the data dictionary construction allows for changes to be accomplished easily and quickly.

A third area of maintenance activities concerns the editing and updating of records in the online databases. These activities include such things as changes in location, circulation status and holding library. These are usually done because a physical unit's status is changed. If the title record as connected to the OCLC number is modified, then the change becomes global. This means that all entries referencing a unique OCLC number reflect the changes as accomplished.

Local editing changes can be extremely useful to the library which is involved in a local system environment. The use of this editing feature must be consistent from record to record and from terminal operator to terminal operator. Local editing can be done by two unique methods at U.A.B.

The first method of local editing is done via the OCLC network and accomplishes two major objectives. One is that it creates our magnetic tape record in the proper form with the proper tags, etc. The second is that it can produce global changes in our local system by modifying the bibliographic information attached to a particular OCLC record number.

This second method of local editing involves the use of the local computer system environment. It is copy specific. As the local database is edited for appropriate information, such as call number or location or holding library, the system reflects an accurate picture of the bibliographic entity as supplied by the shared cataloging system with the appropriate information about each physical piece.

Maintenance of the local database must be responsive to external changes in form, structure and standards. AACR2 is an example of how these changes must be accomplished via the local editing function. Changes in tape format may occur with an external vendor. This is another external change which must be addressed and handled by the local system.

Concerns for the User

Changes in the needs of the user population are also important changes which must be considered by the system designers. The library and the information system exist to meet user needs. The changes may be accomplished technically; however, without adequate training, instruction and communication to the ultimate user, the most technically perfect system may be a disastrous failure. The system must be accurate, instantaneously updated and available to the user population.

There has been much discussion about communication problems and networking. The maintenance of the communications network on the U.A.B. campus is very beneficial to the library user. By maintaining the automated library system on the University's mainframe computer, all terminals on campus have access to the database of library holdings. The technical services staff have benefited greatly from this reality. They can now see a product of their efforts in accurately recording the materials received and added to the collection via the OCLC shared catalog system.

Ensuring Currency

Maintaining the current status of records is an important

part of any system. The local library system allows for withdrawal of material, as well as for the addition of new material. The system must also maintain an accurate record of transactions. These must be monitored by the computer and stored for future reference.

Any system would grow infinitely if purge routines were not designed to remove completed transactions from the databases. This is a maintenance function of great importance, and is often overlooked when systems are initially designed. Because they may initially be overlooked or postponed, purge routines designed as a reaction to growth may not effectively utilize local computer resources, and may not produce a usable product as an end result.

An example of the purge routine is the one used in the acquisitions subsystem. The record entered into the system remains until one of two purge routine criteria are met. The first routine deletes the item from the online database if the record is cancelled. Cancellation may occur before or after the item is placed with a vendor.

Most of the records are completed records. They are purged only ofter certain criteria are satisfied. The final element of the criteria for these records is the date the item was cataloged in OCLC.

In conclusion the librarian must realize that database management and maintenance should be a primary concern in library systems design. Library users, even casual users, will accept without question computerized catalogs and services, so long as they know they can rely on the integrity and currency of the data found therein. We cannot afford to underestimate the value of a well managed and maintained system.

SELECTED BIBLIOGRAPHY

The following bibliography presents readings supplemental to the material covered in the conference program. It is not, nor is it intended to be, comprehensive. Relevant items published prior to 1975, scant in number, are not included. To further limit the scope, only publications related to library tape processing and product development in this country are included. This is not to demean work being accomplished elsewhere, but merely to facilitate the reader's ability to obtain the items cited. A good deal of very valuable information is resident in network newsletters, memoranda, and unpublished library planning documents. Unfortunately, these are usually not indexed, and frequently not easily obtained. Consequently, only a few citations belong to this category. In short, the bibliography is intended to present current, applicable and readily available materials on library archival tape use, processing, and product development.

Aluri, R. *Subject Access to Catalog Records in Large Bibliographic Data Bases.* PhD dissertation. Buffalo: State University of New York, 1981.

Atherton, P.A. *Books Are For Use; Final Report of the Subject Access Project to the Council on Library Resources.* Syracuse, N.Y.: Syracuse University, School of Information Studies, 1978.

Aveney, B. "Tails Wagging Dogs." *Journal of Library Automation.* 14 (March, 1981): 5.

"Bibliographic Specifications for Processing Campus OCLC Records. Division of Library Automation Working Paper, No. 3." *Alternative Catalog Newsletter.* 22–23 (August, 1980): 56–101.

Caplan, E. "Retrospective Duplicate Resolution for the Harvard

Distributable Union Catalog." *Information Technology and Libraries.* 1/2 (June, 1982): 142–143.

Christoffersson, J.G. "Automation at the University of Georgia Libraries." *Journal of Library Automation.* 12 (March, 1979): 22–38.

Crawford, W.C. "Library Standards for Data Structures and Element Identification: US MARC in Theory and Practice." *Library Trends.* 31 (Fall, 1982): 265–281.

Evans, G.T., R. Gifford, and D.R. Franz. *Collection Development Analysis Using OCLC Archival Tapes.* Albany, N.Y.: State University of New York, University Libraries, 1977. ED 152 299.

Fayen, E. *Experimental On-Line Catalog For the Dartmouth College Libraries.* Hanover, N.H.: Dartmouth College Libraries, 1980. ED 190 145.

Hickey, T.B., and D.J. Rypka. "Automatic Detection of Duplicate Monographic Records." *Journal of Library Automation.* 12 (June, 1979): 125–142.

Holley, R.P., and D. Flecker. "Processing OCLC MARC Subscription Tapes at Yale University." *Journal of Library Automation.* 12/1 (March, 1979): 88–91.

Horner, W.C. "Processing OCLC MARC Subscription Tapes at North Carolina State University." *Journal of Library Automation.* 12/1 (March, 1979): 91–94.

Kacala, A. "Routine to Verify Record Lengths and Field Lengths of OCLC Tapes." *Alternative Catalog Newsletter.* 8 (November, 1978): 35–42.

Keslser, B., and D. Shaw. "SOLOS: A Student-Oriented Information Retrieval System Using MARC Records." *Information Technology and Libraries.* 2/3 (September, 1983): 272–279.

Kim, D. "OCLC-MARC Tapes and Collection Management." *Information Technology and Libraries.* 1/1 (March, 1982): 22–27.

Klemperer, K. "Bibliographic Specifications For Consolidation of Records." *Alternative Catalog Newsletter.* 22–23 (August, 1980): 25–55.

MacLaury, K.D. "Automatic Merging of Monographic Data Bases – Use of Fixed Length Keys Derived From Title Strings." *Journal of Library Automation.* 12 (June, 1979): 143–155.

McPherson, D.S., K.E. Coyle, and T.L. Montgomery. "Building a Merged Bibliographic Database: The University of California Experience." *Information Technology and Libraries.* 1/4 (December, 1982): 371–380.

Mandle, P. *SNOBOL4 Program to Manipulate and Search a Sample Library of Congress MARC Tape.* New York: Queens College, 1978.

MDBUPD Replacement Algorithm, Technical Bulletin G102033. Columbus, OH: OCLC, 1977.

Meyer, R.W. and J.F. Knapp. "COM Catalog Based on OCLC Records." *Journal of Library Automation.* 8/4 (December, 1975): 312–321.

Pinzelik, B. *Monitoring Book Losses in a Large Academic Library: Four Methods.* West Lafayette, IN: Purdue University Libraries, 1979. ED 203 852.

Pringle, W.R. "Computing the Effective Lenth of a MARC Tag." *Journal of Library Automation.* 12/4 (December, 1979): 387–390.

"Problems Encountered in Using OCLC Archive Tapes." Berkeley, CA: University of California, Division of Library Automation, 1978.

Reynolds, D. "Entry of Local Data on OCLC: the Options and Their Impact on the Processing of Archival Tapes." *Information Technology and Libraries.* 1/1 (March, 1982): 5–14.

Reynolds, D. "Multi–Institutional Projects Using OCLC Tapes: Some Implications For Cooperative Decision Making on Cataloging Policy." *Action For Libraries.* 6/4 (April, 1981): 1–2.

Reynolds, D. "A Recommended Scheme For Using Indicators

in the 049 Field." *Action For Libraries.* 6/4 (April, 1981): 8-9.

Roth, D. "Innovative Uses of OCLC Records." *Journal of Library Automation.* 11 (June, 1978): 167.

Sawyer, J. "An Archive Tape Processing System For the Triangle Research Libraries Network." *Library Resources & Technical Services.* 26/4 (October/December, 1982): 362-369.

Swanson, D. R. "XMARC: A System for Experimental Indexing and Searching of MARC Records." *Journal of Education for Librarianship.* 20 (Fall, 1979): 91-106.

Williams, M.E., and K.D. MacLaury. "Automatic Merging of Monographic Data Bases -- Identification of Duplicate Records in Multiple Files: The IUCS [IRRL Union Catalog System] Scheme." *Journal of Library Automation.* 12 (June, 1979): 156--168.

Williams, M.E., and Shefner, G.J. "Data Element Statistics for the MARC II Data Base." *Journal of Library Automation.* 9 (June, 1976): 89--100.

Index

AACR2 7, 44, 65, 66, 69, 95, 104, 105, 106, 111
ALA Filing Rules 67
ALIS 79-85
AMIGOS 7
ASCII 7, 19, 20, 39, 45, 81
ASIS see American Society for Information Science
Abbreviations in headings 36
American Society for Information Science 6
American Standard Code for Information Interchange see ASCII
Atlanta Public Library 68
Authority control 7, 66, 69, 74, 85, 87, 95, 105, 106
Autographics, Inc. 87
Automated circulation systems 4, 6, 9, 34, 58, 71-77, 79-85, 87
Automated Library Information System see ALIS
Automatic stamps 37, 73

B/NA see Blackwell/North America
BPI 21, 23, 39
BRS 2
Backup tape 41, 42
Base address 24, 27, 32
Battelle Memorial Laboratories 5
Bibliographic level 24, 27

Binary character 16, 18, 19, 20
Binary-Hex Representation Table 20
Bit 16-18, 22
Blackwell/North America 8
"Bound withs" 75
Bracketed data 34, 37, 72, 81, 95-96
Byte 16-18, 22, 24

CDC Display Code 45
CLSI see CL Systems, Inc.
CL Systems, Inc. 9, 71-74, 76, 87
COBOL 109
COM 4, 6, 7-10, 31, 34-35, 43-45, 48-49, 54-55, 61, 65-69, 81, 87, 103-107
CPI 21, 39, 81
Call number 6, 31, 35, 37, 68, 73, 75-76, 88-93
Carnegie Mellon University 5
Case, Barbara 9
Catline 88
Central State University 9
Character set 19, 21, 45, 73, 83, 94
Circulation control number 100-101
Classed catalog 67, 105
Clemson University 9
Collation 8, 34
Collection development

analyses 4
Collection inventorying 5
Computer output microform see COM
Computer tape 21, 39-40
Control Data Corporation 45
Copyright 5
Cyber computers 45

Dartmouth College 9
Data elements 16-18
Database 16-18
DataPhase 79-85
Delimiter 23-24, 33
Descriptive level 25
Diacritical marks 19, 35, 45, 83-84
Duke University 6, 57

EBCDIC 7, 19-20, 39, 81
EDIT 949 (program) 45, 48, 50, 55
Ellipsis 74
Encoding level 25, 27
End of field mark 33
End of record mark 33
Evans, Glyn 4
Extended Binary Coded Decimal Interchange Code see EBCDIC

FOCUS 87-96
FTU 32
Field 16-18, 21
    Fixed 16-18, 21-22, 24-26, 28, 32-33, 49, 74
    Variable 16-18, 21-23, 26, 28-29, 31, 33
File 16-18
Filing Arrangement in the Library of Congress Catalogs 66
Filing indicators 34, 49, 61-62, 74, 91-92, 103
Fill character 23, 34

Florida Online Computerized User System see FOCUS

Geographic headings 93-94
Georgia Institute of Technology 43-55, 65
Georgia State University 65-69, 103-107

Hex value 19-21, 25, 31, 33
Hickey, Doralyn 1-2
"His, her, its" 35, 104
Holding library codes 35, 37, 49, 76, 88-89, 92-93, 95
Holley, Bob 6
Horner, Bill 6

IBM see International Business Machines
INCOLSA see Indiana Cooperative Library Services Authority
IRG 22-23
ISBD 37, 72
ISBN 21
ISN 76-77
Indiana Cooperative Library Services Authority 6
Indicator count 24, 27
Indicators 33-34, 49, 61-62, 73, 91-92, 103
Input stamps 35-37, 73, 95, 104
International Business Machines 7, 9, 109
Interrecord gap see IRG
Iowa State University 6
Item status records 6, 73

Kim, David 4
Knapp, John 7

LC see Library of Congress
LCCN 26, 33, 77, 83-84, 89
LC-MARC 25-26, 33, 43-44

LCSH see *Library of Congress Subject Headings*
LDR 32
Landau, Herbert B. 2-3
Language codes 34, 62, 92
Library of Congress 5, 10, 16, 62, 88, 103-104
Library of Congress Filing Rules 66
Library of Congress Subject Headings 35, 94, 104, 106
Literal value table 76
Lockheed 2
Logical record 23-24

MARC 5-8, 15-16, 23-24, 26, 33, 36, 38, 42-44, 61, 65, 68, 71-72, 75-77, 80, 84, 94, 110
MARC field tags 5, 27, 49, 68
  001 26, 28, 33, 73
  005 26, 28
  007 26, 28, 94
  008 26, 28-29, 32
  009 26, 28
  010 33
  035 32, 89, 93, 96
  041 34
  049 32, 34, 37, 49, 82, 88-91, 93-95, 101, 104
  050 32, 34, 49, 75, 89, 91
  082 49
  086 49
  09X 37
  090 32, 49, 75, 81, 89, 104
  092 70, 81, 89
  098 35
  099 32, 35-37, 49, 67, 75, 81, 89-91, 104
  1XX 34, 74
  240 36-37, 73
  245 31, 34, 72-74, 91, 103
  300 8, 34, 74
  400 35, 104
  410 35, 104
  411 35, 104
  500 34, 36
  590 32, 34, 37, 104
  6XX 34, 36
  650 35
  69X 35
  87X 44
  910 32, 34, 37, 89
  949 32, 37, 48-50
MARC Formats for Bibliographic Data 16
MARC record structure
  Control fields 24, 26, 28-29
  Directory 24-27, 32-33, 49
  Leader 24-27, 33, 49, 84, 96
  Variable fields 24, 31-35
MARC Tape Input Facility 76-77
Medical Subject Headings 88, 94
Mini-reel 39
Mischo, William 6
Monographic series titles 75
Montana State Library 7

NOTIS 9, 87
National Library of Medicine 88
New York State Library 7
North Carolina State University 6, 57
Northwestern Online Total Integrated System see NOTIS

OCLC 2, 4-10, 15-17, 19, 24,

119

28, 35-36, 39, 43-45, 48, 50, 55, 58-60, 62, 67, 72-76, 78-85, 87, 92-93, 95-96, 99-100, 103-104, 107, 110-111
OCLC-MARC   1, 10, 15-19, 21, 23, 26, 29-31, 34, 38, 43-44, 71, 73
OCLC-MARC Subscription Service Documentation   15, 72
OCLC number   18, 23, 26, 32, 36, 42, 45, 50, 59, 67, 73, 89, 96, 106, 110
  prefix   26, 28, 76
OCLC print program   33, 37, 73, 75, 103-104
OCLC (program)   45
OCLC screen display   15, 24-25, 33, 36, 44, 52, 73, 82, 107
OCLC transaction code   25, 27, 31
  All produce   15, 25
  Cancel   15, 25, 32, 49
  Produce   15, 25, 32, 95-96
  Replace   15, 25, 32, 37, 59
  Update   15, 25, 31-32, 50, 95-96
Ohio State University   9
Online catalogs   4, 34, 57-59, 61, 65, 72, 74, 87
Oral Roberts University   9
Oversize designations   8, 37

Parity bit   21
Pennsylvania State University   9
Physical record   23
Pinzelik, Barbara   5
Position number   32
Pringle, William   5
Print constants   37, 49, 66, 73, 76, 104
Print port interfaces   9, 36
Public Library of Charlotte and Mecklenburg County   79-85
Purdue University   5

RAWDATA (program)   45, 48-50
RLG   see Research Libraries Group
RLIN   see Research Libraries Information Network
Rather, John   66
Reclassification   92-93
Record   16-18
  size   5, 35
  type   24, 27
Recording density   see BPI
Relative position   26
Research Libraries Group   5
Research Libraries Information Network   5-6
Retrospective conversion   4, 6, 7, 31, 34, 80, 87

SOLINET   see Southeastern Library Network
SUNY/OCLC   4
Sawyer, Jeanne   6
Scratch tapes   41
Serials control   32, 58, 87
Serials control local data record   see LDR
Serials holdings lists   4
Series entries   35, 104-105
Southeastern Library Network   4, 7, 39-44, 58, 73, 75-77, 81, 100, 105, 107
Statistics   4, 6-7, 48-50, 62-63,
Subfield codes   24, 33, 49, 82
Subfield count   24, 27
Subject bibliographies   6
Subject headings   35-37, 74, 93-94, 104, 106

TRLN   see Triangle Research Libraries Network
Tape file processing   36, 57
   AMIGOS   7
   Georgia Institute of Technology   43-55
   Southeastern Library Network   4, 7, 39-42, 73, 75-76, 100
   Triangle Research Libraries Network   57-63
Tape library   40
Tarrant County Junior College   9
Tech ID number format   45
Terminal print port   9
Transaction coding   32, 50, 59-61, 63
Transaction date   28
Transaction tables   76, 95
Transaction tape   40
Triangle Research Libraries Network   57-63
Triangle Universities Libraries Cooperative Committee   6

US-MARC   94, 96
Uniform titles   37
University of Alabama in Birmingham   9, 99-102, 109-112
University of California at Los Angeles   9
University of California System   9
University of Florida   87-97
University of Georgia   9
University of Lowell   4
University of Nebraska-Lincoln   9
University of North Carolina-Chapel Hill   6, 57

Validation   61-63
Virginia Polytechnic Institute   9
Volume designations   105

WLN   see Washington Library Network
Washington Library Network   5, 7
Winthrop College   71-77
Wrightline seal   40
Write-ring   40

"x" call number suppression   31, 75

Yale University   6